Selections From the Poetical Works of Richard Monckton Milnes

SELECTIONS

FROM THE

POETICAL WORKS

OF

RICHARD MONCKTON MILNES,

LORD HOUGHTON.

SELECTIONS

FROM THE

POETICAL WORKS

OF

RICHARD MONCKTON MILNES,

LORD HOUGHTON.

LONDON:

JOHN MURRAY, ALBEMARLE STREET.

1863.

LONDON:
BRADBURY AND EVANS, PRINTERS, WHITEFRIARS.

CONTENTS.

———◦┼❉┼◦———

POEMS OF SENTIMENT AND REFLECTION.

PALM LEAVES.

OCCASIONAL POEMS.

MEMORIALS OF TRAVEL.

POEMS.—LEGENDARY AND HISTORICAL.

POEMS

OF

SENTIMENT AND REFLECTION.

————◦•✦•◦————

UNSPOKEN DIALOGUE.

ABOVE the trailing mignonnette
 That dressed the window-sill,
A Lady watched, with lips firm-set,
 And looks of earnest will:
Four decades o'er her life had met,
 And left her lovely still.

Not to the radiant firmament,
 Not to the garden's grace,
The courses of her mind were bent,—
 But where, with sweetest face,
Forth from the other window leant,
 The Daughter of the place.

Thus ran her thoughts: "O, wretched day!
 When She was born so fair;
Well could I let my charms decay,
 If she were not their heir:
I loathe the sunbeams as they play
 About her golden hair.

B

" Yet why ?   She is too good—too mild—
  So madly to aspire—
He is no Boy to be beguiled
  By sparks of coloured fire ;
I will not dream a pretty child
  Can mar my deep desire.

" Her fatherless and lonely days
  Are sere before their time ;
In scenes of gaiety and praise
  She will regain her prime,
And cease to haunt these wooded ways,
  With sentimental rhyme."

On to the conscious maiden past
  Those words without the tongue ;
Half-petulantly back she cast
  The glistening curls that hung
About her neck, and answered fast,
  " Yes, I am young—too young.

" Yet am I graver than my wont,
  Graver when He is here ;
Beneath the glory of his front
  I tremble—not with fear,
But, as I read, Bethesda's font
  Felt with the Angel near.

" Must I mate only with my kind,
  With something as unwise
As my poor self, and never find
  Affection I can prize
At once with an adoring mind,
  And with admiring eyes ?

"My mother trusts to drag me down
　To some low range of life,
By pleasures of the clamo'rous town,
　And vanity's mean strife ;
And in such selfish tumult drown
　My hope to be *his* wife."

Then darker round the Lady grew
　The meditative cloud,—
And stormy thoughts began to brew
　She dared not speak aloud,
For then, without disguise, she knew
　That rivalry avowed.

"What is my being, if I lose
　My love's last stake ? while She
Has the fair future where to choose
　Her woman's destiny,
Free scope those means and powers to use
　Which Time denies to me.

"Was it for this her baby arms
　About my neck were flung?
Was it for this I found such charms
　In her uncertain tongue?
Was it for this those vain alarms
　My mother-soul unstrung?

"O horrible ! to wish my child—
　My sole one left—unborn,
And, seeing her so meek and mild,
　To hold such gifts in scorn :
My nature is grown waste and wild,
　My heart with fury torn."

Speechless—enchanted to the spot—
　The girl could scarce divine
The whole disaster of her lot ;
　But, without sound or sign,
She cried, " O, mother !　Love him not—
　O, let his love be mine !

" You have had years of full delight—
　Your girlhood's passion-dream
Was realized to touch and sight,
　As bright as it could seem ;
And now you interpose, like night,
　Before my life's first gleam.

" Yet You were once what I am now,
　You won your maiden prize—
You told me of my Father—how
　You lived but in his eyes :
You spoke of the perpetual vow,
　The troth that never dies.

" Dear mother !　dearer, kinder, far,
　If by my childhood's bed
Your care had never strove to bar
　Misfortune from my head,
But laid me where my brothers are,
　Among the quiet dead.

" Ah !　why not die ?　This cruel strife
　Can thus—thus only—cease.
Dear Lord !　take home this erring life,
　This struggling soul release ;
From Heaven, perchance, upon *his* wife,
　I might look down in peace."

That prayer, like some electric flame,
　　Struck with resistless force
The Lady's agitated frame;
　　Nor halted in its course
Till her hard pride was turned to shame,
　　Her passion to remorse.

She spoke—her words were very low—
　　But resolute in tone;
"Dear child!—He comes—nay, blush not so
　　To have your secret known,
'Tis best—'tis best that I should go—
　　And leave you here alone."

Then, as his steps grew near and fast,
　　Her hand was on the door,
Her heart, by holy grace, had cast
　　The demon from its core,—
And on the threshold calm she past
　　The Man she loved no more.

———

NEVER RETURN!

IT was a meeting, such as on this earth
The bonds of time and circumstances permit
Rarely to those who feel and think as one:
A small but "sacred band" wholly made up
Of lovers—of old friends who had not met
For many weary years—of some whose names
Had to each other been familiar sounds,
And who now felt their spirits meet and join
At once, like waters—and of four who formed　ʋ

Two complete beings, man and woman blent,
Ensamples of connubial unity.

This wondrous concert of internal life
Went on beneath the open infinite
Of an Italian sky, that varied not
More than the peace that dwelt within their souls;
So that when, all at once, before their eyes
The lake grew less transparent, and the leaves
Of the pale olive less distinguishable,
And the hills glow'd like metal, while the snow
First turn'd to gold, then red, then deadly white,
They were astonished at the flight of time
That had not struck one hour within their hearts;
And amid all the riches of that South
They grudged the North its solitary charm
Of long, long, twilight, mourning bitterly
That here the day was ravished from their eyes
And bore a world of bliss along with it.
At last one rose, one younger than the rest,
One before whom life lay a glorious stream
Flowing, by right divine, through pleasant lands,
Unconscious of the fatal final sea.
He stood irradiate with that rosy light,
The funeral banner of the fallen sun,
Most like an image of incarnate Hope,
From whom no night can hide the coming morn.

Raising one arm in ecstasy, he cried,—
" Before we leave this consecrated spot,
Before this Day of Days is wholly dead,
Before the dew obliterates all our steps
From this light earth, let us record a vow !
Let us, in presence of these lasting hills,
In presence of this day's delicious thoughts,
That yet are hardly memory,—let us pledge

Our hearts together, that on this same day
Each rolling year shall see us meet again
In this same place, as far as Fate allows.
Some may be held away by cruel chance,
Some by the great divorcer, none by choice ;
And thus, at least for a large lapse of time,
One Day shall stand apart from other days,
Birth-day of inward Life—Love's Holyday—
The Wedding-day, not of one single pair,
But of a thousand thoughts, and hopes, and joys,—
The Saint's-day, in whose fair recurrent round
Each year will circle all its blessedness."

    With more than ready welcome, with loud glee,
Was hailed this happy fancy ; each was prompt
To press the other's hand, and, joining round
The founder of this mighty festival,
To seal the sudden contract—all save One.

    This one had gazed on the impassioned youth
With tender looks, that to the rest had seemed
Fond sympathy,—but had far other sense.
And now he spoke, at first with trem'lous voice,
Softened, as if it passed through inner tears.
" O Friends ! dear Friends ! do anything but this :
This is a deed to wake the jealous gods
Into a cruel vengeance. We are Men ;
We live from hour to hour, and have no right,
Holding no power, to fetter future years.
We may, if Heaven so please, preserve our loves,
We may enjoy our interchange of souls
Long, and in many shapes of time and fate ;
But to this spot, the scene of this To-day,
Let us, whate'er befall, never return !

    " Never return ! If hitherward your path
Should chance to lie, when seeking other lands,

Spare not the time it takes to circuit round
This scene, and gaze upon its face no more.
Say, if you will, 'It lies amid the gold
The sunset spreads beyond that purple ridge;'
Say, if you will, 'The atoms of this stream
Flow through the place I value most on earth,
And bear my yearning heart along with them;'
Say, if you will, 'There rests my Paradise;'
But there, whate'er befall, never return!
"Never return! Should we come back, dear Friend!
As you implore us, *we* should not return:
Came we all back, as Heaven would hardly grant,
There must be faded cheeks and sunken eyes,
And minds enfeebled with the rack of time,
And hearts grown colder, and, it may be, cold.
The sun might shine as gorgeous as this noon,
And yet find clouds between it and our souls;
The lake might rest like light upon the earth,
And but reflect to us sweet faces gone
And pictures mournful as the dead below;
The very flowers might breathe a poisonous breath
Should we, led by false hope, ever return!
"Trust not the dear palladium of the Past
Upon the Future's breast. The Past is ours,
And we can build a temple of rare thoughts,
Adorned with all affection's tracery,
In which to keep from contact vile and rude
The grace of this incomparable Day.
We may, by heart, go through it all again;
We may, with it, give colour, warmth, and form
To the black, shapeless mountains far away—
Calm down the seething, hyperborean, waves
To the pure sapphire of this lake, and spread
Rose-trellises across the gloomy front

Of blank old dwellings in the distant town;
But we must keep the vision fresh as morn,—
We must not risk that it should ever lose
One of its features of staid loveliness,
One of its sweet associated thoughts.—
Therefore, whate'er befall, never return!
   "Never return! Time writes these little words
On palace and on hamlet; strife is vain;
First-love returns not,—friendship comes not back,—
Glory revives not. Things are given us once,
And only once; yet we may keep them ours,
If, like this day, we take them out of time,
And make them portions of the constant peace
Which is the shadow of eternity!"
   So ended the serene Philosopher;
And to all minds the sad persuasive truth
Found an immediate access: the poor youth,
Whose spirit was but now a-fire with hope,
Cast down his quenched enthusiastic eyes.
"Never return!" in many various tones,
All grave, yet none wholly disconsolate,
Was echoed, amid parting signs of love,
As they went on their common homeward way.
Silent above, the multitudinous stars
Said, "We are steadfast,—we are not as Ye."
Silent the fields, up to the phantom hills,
Said, "We are dreaming of the vanished days
Which we shall see again, but Ye no more."
So heavy pressed the meditative calm
On those full hearts, that all rejoiced to hear
The shrill cicala, clittering from below,
Call on the fire-flies dancing through the vines.

PARTED AND MET.

I.

I KNOW not, whether such great power
Is in despair,—it may be so,—
But, Myrrha! ere this ebbing hour
Is over, I will try to go :
Once more the glory of your form
Shall fall upon my path,—once more !
And fear not lest the inner storm
Should burst the bounds it kept before.

I have one last, light, boon to pray—
Do not be mercilessly kind ;
Hold back your hand, and turn away
Those splendours I must leave behind ;
Or arm your eyes with chilly glare,
(Though wont to be so burning-bright)
Like their far sisters of the air,
Which light, but cannot warm, the night.

But most of all, I could not bear
From you that mocking word, "Farewell !"—
How well my riven heart will fare,
I think I have not now to tell.
Be silent, passionless—the ghost
Of your own self—a solemn shade,
Whose form, to others wholly lost,
In my deep soul, as in a grave, is laid.

II.

My spirit staggered at the sight,
So painful and so strange,
I could not think that years had might
To work such fearful change ;
And ere I ceased from wondering,
My tears fell fast and free,
That wretched, stricken, hopeless thing,—
I dared not call it Thee.

If I had heard that thou wert dead,
I hastily had cried,
"She was so richly favourèd,
God must forgive her pride ;
My heart lay withered, while the crown
Of life was fresh upon her,—
I linger still, she has gone down
In beauty and in honour."

But now, to see thy living death,—
Power, glory, arts, all gone,—
Thy empire lost, and thy poor breath
Still vainly struggling on !
Alas ! a thought of saddest weight
Presses and will have vent :
"Had she not scorned my love,—her fate
Had been so different !

"Had her heart bent its haughty will
To take me for its lord,
She had been proudly happy still,
Still honoured, still adored ;

The weak love-ties of face and frame
Time easily may sever,
But I had thought her still the same,
As beautiful as ever.

"She had then felt no shame or sorrow,
At seeing fall away
The slaves who mock the god to-morrow,
They worshipped all day ;
While I preserved, with honest truth,
Through every varying stage,
Her image which adorned my youth,
To glorify my age."

And do not treat this thought as light,
Nor ask with taunting sign,
"Has then thy life-course been so bright
That thou canst scorn at mine?"
Myrrha! the name of Misery
Is clear upon my brow,
Yet am I not, nor e'er can be,
So lorn a thing as Thou.

He, who for Love has undergone
The worst that can befall,
Is happier thousand-fold than one
Who never loved at all ;
A grace within his soul has reigned,
Which nothing else can bring—
Thank God for all that I have gained,
By that high suffering !

FAMILIAR LOVE.

WE read together, reading the same book,
Our heads bent forward in a half-embrace,
So that each shade that either spirit took
Was straight reflected in the other's face :
We read, not silent, nor aloud,—but each
Followed the eye that past the page along,
With a low murmu'ring sound that was not speech,
    Yet with so much monotony,
    In its half-slumbering harmony,
    You might not call it song ;
    More like a bee, that in the noon rejoices,
Than any customed mood of human voices.
Then if some wayward or disputed sense
Made cease awhile that music, and brought on
A strife of gracious-worded difference,
Too light to hurt our soul's dear unison,
We had experience of a blissful state,
In which our powers of thought stood separate,
Each in its own high freedom, set apart,
But both close folded in one loving heart ;
So that we seemed, without conceit, to be
Both one and two in our identity.

We prayed together, praying the same prayer,
But each that prayed did seem to be alone,
And saw the other, in a golden air
Poised far away, beneath a vacant throne,

Becko'ning the kneeler to arise and sit
Within the glory which encompassed it :
And when obeyed, the Vision stood beside,
And led the way through the' upper hyaline,
Smiling in beauty tenfold glorified,
Which, while on earth, had seemed enough divine,
The beauty of the Spirit-Bride,
Who guided the rapt Florentine.

The depth of human reason must become
As deep as is the holy human heart,
Ere aught in written phrases can impart
The might and meaning of that extasy
To those low souls, who hold the mystery
Of the' unseen universe for dark and dumb.

But we were mortal still, and when again
We raised our bended knees, I do not say
That our descending spirits felt no pain
To meet the dimness of an earthly day ;
Yet not as those disheartened, and the more
Debased the higher that they rose before,
But, from the exaltation of that hour,
Out of God's choicest treasu'ry, bringing down
New virtue to sustain all ill,—new power
To braid Life's thorns into a regal crown,
We past into the outer world, to prove
The strength miracu'lous of united Love.

STRANGERS YET.

STRANGERS yet!
After years of life together,
After fair and stormy weather,
After travel in far lands,
After touch of wedded hands,—
Why thus joined? Why ever met,
If they must be strangers yet?

Strangers yet!
After childhood's winning ways,
After care and blame and praise,
Counsel asked and wisdom given,
After mutual prayers to Heaven,
Child and parent scarce regret
When they part—are strangers yet.

Strangers yet!
After strife for common ends—
After title of " old friends,"
After passions fierce and tender,
After cheerful self-surrender,
Hearts may beat and eyes be met,
And the souls be strangers yet.

Strangers yet!
Oh! the bitter thought to scan
All the loneliness of man :—

Nature, by magnetic laws,
Circle unto circle draws,
But they only touch when met,
Never mingle—strangers yet.

Strangers yet !
Will it evermore be thus—
Spirits still impervious ?
Shall we never fairly stand
Soul to soul as hand to hand ?
Are the bounds eternal set
To retain us—strangers yet ?

Strangers yet !
Tell not Love it must aspire
Unto something other—higher :
God himself were loved the best
Were our sympathies at rest,
Rest above the strain and fret
Of the world of—strangers yet !
Strangers yet !

———

A RECOLLECTION.

I KNEW that I should be his bride,
  And to my tearful eyes
Lay that fair future, half descried
  Through a divine surprise :
I knew that I should be his wife,
  And that his arm would bend
Around me down the walks of life,
  As friend sustaining friend :

And yet when I beheld him there,
  Amid a joyous throng,
Amid the witty and the fair,
  Who knew and prized him long,—
Amid the comrades of his youth,
  The kinsmen of his line,
I almost faltered at the truth
  With which I called him mine.

I saw they thought that I was proud
  To claim him as mine own,
While all my being inly bowed
  As with a weight unknown.
For if I dared my heart to place
  Above its own just meed,
I might be distanced in a race
  In which the strong succeed !

But now that years have rolled away,
  A variegated stream,
And, one by one, that bright array
  Has vanished like a dream ;
Now that the very name of wife
  Has higher titles earned,
I smile to ponder on that strife
  Of feelings undiscerned.

Ah ! had I known him but as they,
  How weary might have been
The intercourse of every day,
  The rarely-changing scene,—

The life that over-long may prove
    For passion or for power,
But too, too, short for that still love
    Which blesses every hour.

RAPTURE.

BECAUSE, from all that round Thee move,
Planets of Beauty, Strength, and Grace,
I am elected to Thy love,
And have my home in Thy embrace ;
I wonder all men do not see
The crown that Thou hast set on me.

Because, when, prostrate at Thy feet,
Thou didst emparadise my pain,—
Because Thy heart on mine has beat,
Thy head within my hands has lain,
I am transfigured, by that sign,
Into a being like to Thine.

The mirror from its glossy plain
Receiving still returns the light,
And, being generous of its gain,
Augments the very solar might :
What unreflected light would be,
Is just Thy spirit without me.

Thou art the flame, whose rising spire
In the dark air sublimely sways,
And I the tempest that swift fire
Gathers at first and then obeys :

All that was Thine ere we were wed
Have I by right inherited.

Is life a stream?   Then from Thy hair
One rosebud on the current fell,
And straight it turned to crystal there,
As adamant immovable :
Its steadfast place shall know no more
The sense of after and before.

Is life a plant?   The King of years
To mine nor good nor ill can bring ;—
Mine grows no more ; no more it fears
Even the brushing of his wing :
With sheathèd scythe I see him go,—
I have no flowers that *he* can mow.

THE TREASURE-SHIP.

My heart is freighted full of love,
As full as any argosy,
With gems below and gems above,
And ready for the open sea ;
For the wind is blowing summerly.

Full strings of nature's beaded pearl,
Sweet tears ! composed in amorous ties
And turkis-lockets, that no churl
Hath fashioned out mechanic-wise,
But all made up of thy blue eyes.

And girdles wove of subtle sound,
And thoughts not trusted to the air,
Of antique mould,—the same as bound,
In Paradise, the primal pair,
Before Love's arts and niceness were.

And carcanets of living sighs ;
Gums that have dropped from Love's own stem,
And one small jewel most I prize—
The darling gaud of all of them—
I wot, so rare and fine a gem
Ne'er glowed on Eastern anadem.

I've cased the rubies of thy smiles,
In rich and triply-plated gold ;
But *this* no other wealth defiles,
Itself itself can only hold—
The stealthy kiss on Maple-wold.

FRIENDSHIP AND LOVE.

IF I could coldly sum the love
That we each other bear,
My heart would to itself disprove
The truth of what was there ;—
Its willing utterance should express
Nothing but joy and thankfulness.

Yet Friendship is so blurred a name,
A good so ill-discerned,
That if the nature of the flame
That in our bosoms burned
Were treasured in becoming rhymes,
It might have worth in after-times.

The Lover is a God,—the ground
He treads on is not ours;
His soul by other laws is bound,
Sustained by other powers;
We, children of a lowlier lot,
Listen and understand him not.

Liver of a diviner life,
He turns a vacant gaze
Toward the theatre of strife,
Where we consume our days;
His own and that one other heart
Form for himself a world apart:

A sphere, whose sympathies are wings,
On which he rests sublime,
Above the shifts of casual things,
Above the flow of time;
How should he feel, how can he know
The sense of what goes on below?

Reprove him not,—no selfish aim
Here leads to selfish ends;
You might as well the infant blame
That smiles to grieving friends:
Could all thus love, and love endure,
Our world would want no other cure.

But few are the elect, for whom
This fruit is on the stem,—
And for that few an early tomb
Is open,—not for them,
But for their love; for they live on,
Sorrow and shame! when Love is gone:

They who have dwelt at Heaven's own gate,
And felt the light within,
Come down to our poor mortal state,
Indifference, care, and sin ;
And their dimmed spirits hardly bear
A trace to tell what once they were.

Fever and Health their thirst may slake
At one and the same stream ;
The dreamer knows not till he wake
The falsehood of his dream :
How, *while* I love thee, can I prove
The surer nature of our love ?

It is, that while our choicest hours
Are closed from vulgar ken,
We daily use our active powers,—
Are men to brother men,—
It is, that, with our hands in one,
We do the work that should be done.

Our hands in one, we will not shrink
From life's severest due,—
Our hands in one, we will not blink
The terrible and true ;
What each would feel a heavy blow
Falls on us both as autumn snow.

The simple unpresumptuous sway,
By which our hearts are ruled,
Contains no seed of self-decay ;
Too temperate to be cooled,
Our Passion fears no blast of ill,
No winter, till the one last chill.

And even then no frantic grief
Shall shake the mourner's mind,—
He will reject no small relief
Kind Heaven may leave behind,
Nor set at nought his bliss enjoyed,
When now by human fate alloyed.

———

THE FLOWER OF FRIENDSHIP.

WHEN first the Friendship-flower is planted
Within the garden of your soul,
Little of care or thought is wanted
To guard its beauty fresh and whole ;
But when the full empassioned age
Has well revealed the magic bloom,
A wise and holy tutelage
Alone avoids the open tomb.

It is not Absence you should dread,—
For Absence is the very air
In which, if sound at root, the head
Shall wave most wonderful and fair :
With sympathies of joy and sorrow
Fed, as with morn and even dews,
Ideal colouring it may borrow
Richer than ever earthly hues.

But oft the plant, whose leaves unsere
Refresh the desert, hardly brooks
The common-peopled atmosphere
Of daily thoughts and words and looks ;

It trembles at the brushing wings
Of many' a careless fashion-fly,
And strange suspicions aim their stings
To taint it as they wanton by.

Rare is the heart to bear a flower,
That must not wholly fall and fade,
Where alien feelings, hour by hour,
Spring up, beset, and overshade ;
Better, a child of care and toil,
To glorify some needy spot,
Than in a glad redundant soil
To pine neglected and forgot.

Yet when, at last, by human slight,
Or close of their permitted day,
From the bright world of life and light
Such fine creations lapse away,—
Bury the relics that retain
Sick odours of departed pride,—
Hoard, as ye will, your memory's gain,
But leave the blossoms where they died.

———

FAIR-WEATHER FRIEND.

BECAUSE I mourned to see thee fall
From where I mounted thee,
Because I did not find thee all
I feigned a friend should be ;
Because things are not what they seem,
And this our world is full of dream,—

Because thou lovest sunny weather,
Am I to lose thee altogether ?

I know harsh words have found their way,
Which I would fain recall ;
And angry passions had their day,
But now—forget them all ;
Now that I only ask to share
Thy presence, like some pleasant air,
Now that my gravest thoughts will bend
To thy light mind, fair-weather friend !

See ! I am careful to atone
My spirit's voice to thine ;
My talk shall be of mirth alone,
Of music, flowers, and wine !
I will not breathe an earnest breath,
I will not think of life or death,
I will not dream of any end,
While thou art here, fair-weather friend !

Delusion brought me only woe,
I take thee as thou art ;
Let thy gay verdure overgrow
My deep and serious heart !
Let me enjoy thy laugh, and sit
Within the radiance of thy wit,
And lean where'er thy humours tend,
Taking fair weather from my friend.

Or, if I see my doom is traced
By fortune's sterner pen,
And pain and sorrow must be faced,—
Well, thou canst leave me then ;

And fear not lest some faint reproach
Should on thy happy hours encroach ;
Nay, blessings on thy steps attend,
Where'er they turn, fair-weather friend !

———

PAST FRIENDSHIP.

WE that were friends, yet are not now,
   We that must daily meet
With ready words and courteous bow,
   Acquaintance of the street ;
We must not scorn the holy past,
   We must remember still
To honour feelings that outlast
   The reason and the will.

I might reprove thy broken faith,
   I might recall the time
When thou wert chartered mine till death,
   Through every fate and clime ;
When every letter was a vow,
   And fancy was not free
To dream of ended love ; and thou
   Wouldst say the same of me.

No, no, 'tis not for us to trim
   The balance of our wrongs,
Enough to leave remorse to him
   To whom remorse belongs !
Let our dead friendship be to us
   A desecrated name,
Unutterable, mysterious,
   A sorrow and a shame.

A sorrow that two souls which grew
   Encased in mutual bliss,
Should wander, callous strangers, through
   So cold a world as this !
A shame that we, whose hearts had earned
   For life an early heaven,
Should be like angels self-returned
   To Death, when once forgiven !

Let us remain as living signs,
   Where they that run may read
Pain and disgrace in many lines
   As of a loss indeed ;
That of our fellows any who
   The prize of love have won
May tremble at the thought to do
   The thing that we have done !

NOT TO-MORROW!

O TERRIBLE To-morrow ! that will come
On me, alone and far away from Her,
Who was my day, to-day, and every day :
To-morrow she will not be by my side,
And not to-morrow is as never more.

As the poor Soul, that images itself
Parted from God, its Father, and its Cause,
Finds in that very parting all its sin,
And in that very parting knows itself
Evil and reprobate, and will not hear
A single utterance of intrinsic hope :

So to my heart the world to-come is blank,
And not to-morrow is as never more.

I will not sound the possibilities :
I will not ask whether in some far time,
In some far order of the Universe,
In some far destination of myself,
We may not meet again? I only know
The burden of one thought that bears me down :
And that to-morrow is as never more.

Ever and Never—foolish play of words—
Dancing before the finite mind of man :
Our Ever is a sweet successive dream
Of wavelets, over which the bounding heart
Goes forward 'mid the shoals and rocks of Time,
Until it crashes on the fronting shore :
Our Never is the Present without Hope,
And my next moment is as never more.

Let the serene Philosopher sit down,
Knowing that sorrow is the gift of God,
And bid the streams of consolation flow
Through the dim arid future : so have I
Striven in my time, and conquered in the end.
But how can it be good for me to lose
My better self, my moral sustenance,
One whom I followed in a heaven-ward path,
To which I now can see no other clue ?
How can it make me better to be shorn
Of that within me that can claim to be
More than the crystal shining in the rock,
More than the blossom withering at my feet ?
How can a man be wiser, if he lose

All sense that makes the difference between
This place and that, this circumstance and that,
Between to-morrow's life and never more?

I know to-morrow will be as to-day,—
Sun-rise—birds' chirp—the stolid hours roll on,
Careless of what they crush—without a thought
That in the world there is a man the less,
A mind the less to' engender noble deeds,
A heart the less to beat for other men,
A soul the less to claim eternal life,—
For whom to-morrow is as never more.

What is the presence of continuous pain,
Some sharper and some better to be borne,
Calling out courage in the patient man,
Matched with this absence of the power to love,
This loss of that within which can stand up
In the broad face of Heaven, and say, "'Tis I,
Living and suffering for some secret end
Of the mysterious Master of us all:"
Is it that I have given away Myself,
And know not where to look for it again
In any corner of the field of Time,
While Not to-morrow is as Never more?

HALF TRUTH.

THE words that trembled on your lips
Were uttered not—I know it well;
The tears that would your eyes eclipse
Were checked and smothered, ere they fell:

The looks and smiles I gained from you
Were little more than others won,
And yet you are not wholly true,
Nor wholly just what you have done.

You know, at least you might have known,
That every little grace you gave,—
Your voice's somewhat lowered tone,—
Your hand's faint shake or parting wave,—
Your every sympathetic look
At words that chanced your soul to touch,
While reading from some favourite book,
Were much to me—alas, how much !

You might have seen—perhaps you saw—
How all of these were steps of hope
On which I rose, in joy and awe,
Up to my passion's lofty scope ;
How after each, a firmer tread
I planted on the slippery ground,
And higher raised my ventur'ous head,
And ever new assurance found.

May be, without a further thought,
It only pleased you thus to please,
And thus to kindly feelings wrought
You measured not the sweet degrees ;
Yet, though you hardly understood
Where I was following at your call,
You might—I dare to say you should—
Have thought how far I had to fall.

And thus when fallen, faint, and bruised,
I see another's glad success,
I may have wrongfully accused
Your heart of vulgar fickleness :
But even now, in calm review
Of all I lost and all I won,
I cannot deem you wholly true,
Nor wholly just what you have done.

———

RESTORE.

'TWOULD seem the world were large enough to hold
    Both me and thee :
But now I find in space by thee controlled
    No room for me.

We portioned all between us, as was fair ;
    That time is past ;
And now I would recover my lost share,
    Which still thou hast.

For that old love on which we both did live,—
    Keep it who can !
Yet give me back the love I used to give
    To God and man.

Give me my young ambition,—my fresh fire
    Of high emprize ;
Give me the sweet indefinite desire
    That lit mine eyes :—

Give me my sense of pleasure ;—give me all
    My range of dreams ;
Give me my power at sunset to recall
    The noontide's beams ;

If not my smiles, at least give back my tears,
    And leave me free
To weep that all which man and nature cheers
    Is lost with thee !

———

THE LETTERS OF YOUTH.

LOOK at the leaves I gather up in trembling,—
Little to see, and sere, and time-bewasted,
But they are other than the tree can bear now,
    For they are mine !

Deep as the tumult in an archèd sea-cave,
Out of the Past these antiquated voices
Fall on my heart's ear ; I must listen to them,
    For they are mine !

Whose is this hand that wheresoe'er it wanders,
Traces in light words thoughts that come as lightly ?
Who was the king of all this soul-dominion ?
    I ? Was it mine ?

With what a healthful appetite of spirit,
Sits he at Life's inevitable banquet,
Tasting delight in every thing before him !
    Could this be mine ?

See ! how he twists his coronals of fancy,
Out of all blossoms, knowing not the poison,—
How his young eye is meshed in the enchantment !
       And it was mine !

What, is this I ?—this miserable complex,
Losing and gaining, only knit together
By the ever-bursting fibres of remembrance,—
       What is this *mine ?*

Surely we *are* by feeling as by knowing,—
Changing our hearts our being changes with them ;
Take them away,—these spectres of my boyhood,
       They are not mine.

ONE-SIDED TROTH.

IT is not for what He would be to me now,
If he still were here, that I mourn him so :
It is for the thought of a broken vow,
And for what he was to me long ago.

Strange, while he lived and moved upon earth,
Though I would not, and could not, have seen him again,
His being to me had an infinite worth,
And the void of his loss is an infinite pain.

I had but to utter his name, and my youth
Rose up in my soul, and my blood grew warm ;
And I hardly remembered the broken truth,
And I wholly remembered the ancient charm.

                     D

I watched the' unfolding scenes of his life,
From' the lonely retreat where my heart reposed ;
'Twas a magical drama—a fabulous strife ;
Now' the curtain has fallen, the volume is closed.

The sense of my very self grows dim,
With nothing but Self either here or beyond ;
That Self which would have been lost in him,
Had he only died ere he broke the bond.

————

TO SORROW.

SISTER Sorrow ! sit beside me,
Or, if I must wander, guide me ;
Let me take thy hand in mine,
Cold alike are mine and thine.

Think not, Sorrow, that I hate thee,—
Think not I am frightened at thee,—
Thou art come for some good end,
I will treat thee as a friend.

I will say that thou art bound
My unshielded soul to wound
By some force without thy will
And art tender-minded still.

I will say thou givest scope
To the breath and light of hope ;
That thy gentle tears have weight
Hardest hearts to penetrate :

That thy shadow brings together
Friends long lost in sunny weather,
With an hundred offices
Beautiful and blest as these.

Softly takest Thou the crown
From my haughty temples down ;
Place it on thine own pale brow,
Pleasure wears one,—why not Thou ?

Let the blossoms glisten there
On thy long unbanded hair,
And when I have borne my pain,
Thou wilt give them me again.

If Thou goest, sister Sorrow !
I shall look for Thee to-morrow,—
I shall often see Thee drest
As a masquerading guest :

And howe'er Thou hid'st the name,
I shall know Thee still the same
As Thou sitt'st beside me now,
With my garland on thy brow.

THE LONG-AGO.

Eyes which can but ill define
Shapes that rise about and near,
Through the far horizon's line
Stretch a vision free and clear :

D 2

Memories feeble to retrace
Yesterday's immediate flow,
Find a dear familiar face
In each hour of Long-ago.

Follow yon majestic train
Down the slopes of old renown,
Knightly forms without disdain,
Sainted heads without a frown ;
Emperors of thought and hand
Congregate, a glorious show,
Met from every age and land
In the plains of Long-ago.

As the heart of childhood brings
Something of eternal joy,
From its own unsounded springs,
Such as life can scarce destroy :
So, remindful of the prime,
Spirits, wand'ring to and fro,
Rest upon the resting time
In the peace of Long-ago,

Youthful Hope's religious fire,
When it burns no longer, leaves
Ashes of impure Desire
On the altars it bereaves ;
But the light that fills the Past
Sheds a still diviner glow,
Ever farther it is cast
O'er the scenes of Long-ago.

Many a growth of pain and care,
Cumbering all the present hour,
Yields, when once transplanted there,
Healthy fruit or pleasant flower ;
Thoughts that hardly flourish here,
Feelings long have ceased to blow,
Breathe a native atmosphere
In the world of Long-ago.

On that deep-retiring shore
Frequent pearls of beauty lie,
Where the passion-waves of yore
Fiercely beat and mounted high :
Sorrows that are sorrows still
Lose the bitter taste of woe ;
Nothing's altogether ill
In the griefs of Long-ago.

Tombs where lonely love repines,
Ghastly tenements of tears,
Wear the look of happy shrines
Through the golden mist of years :
Death, to those who trust in good,
Vindicates his hardest blow ;
Oh ! we would not, if we could,
Wake the sleep of Long-ago !

Though the doom of swift decay
Shocks the soul where life is strong,
Though for frailer hearts the day
Lingers sad and overlong,—

Still the weight will find a leaven,
Still the spoiler's hand is slow,
While the Future has its Heaven,
And the Past its Long-ago.

————

SIMPLE SOUNDS.

O POWER! whose organ is the tremulous air,
Thou that not only to the accordant sense
Unfoldest all a world of harsh and fair,
But hast a far diviner influence,
Submitting to inscrutable controul
The finest elements of human soul ;

O mystic Sound! what heart can keep aloof,
If summoned to acknowledge thy bland sway,
As thou approachest in the golden woof
Of luscious harmonies serene or gay?
But thou hast moods I would not honour less,
Thy simplest forms of moral kingliness.

How did my childish ecstasy burst out,
When first I found thy Echoes at my call!
What blithe caprice of whisper, song, and shout,
Woke the steep hill and challenged the long wall!
How we *did* laugh! I needed from that day
Nor other playfellows nor other play.

Further in life, when thoughts and feelings slept
In my heart's tomb, some one particular tone
Of common bells has stung me till I wept,
And rushed away, oppressed by things foregone ;

For though the hours recalled be bright and glad,
Still earnest memory ever will be sad.

When late I changed the still unpeopled air
Of the clear South for this my mother clime,
I quivered with delight, as every where
Sweet birds in happy snatches hailed the prime ;
A throstle's twitter made old walks arise,
With lilac-bunches dancing in my eyes.

What love we, about those we love the best,
Better than their dear voices ?   At what cost
Would one not gather to an aching breast
Each little word of some whom we have lost ?
And oh ! how blank to hear, in some far place,
A voice we know, and see a stranger's face.

I never hold my truth to God more leal
Than when it thunders ; that monotonous roll
Has after-lightning potent to reveal
Many dark words on Faith's sin-shaded scroll :
Talk with a stormy sky, man ! prone to deem
That nothing is, because of thine own Dream.

And now within the hush of evening waves,
Cast by light force upon a shingly shore,
My Spirit rests ; the ruins and fresh graves
That strewed its earthly path here vex no more :
Rocked on the soothing surge, its life is all
One soft attraction and one mellow fall.

A PRAYER.

EVIL, every living hour,
Holds us in its wilful hand,
Save as Thou, essential Power!
May'st be gracious to withstand:
Pain within the subtle flesh,
Heavy lids that cannot close,
Hearts that Hope will not refresh,—
Hand of healing! interpose!

Tyranny's strong breath is tainting
Nature's sweet and vivid air,
Nations silently are fainting
Or up-gather in despair:
Not to those distracted wills
Trust the judgment of their woes;
While the cup of anguish fills,
Arm of Justice! interpose!

Pleasures night and day are hovering
Round their prey of weary hours;
Weakness and unrest discovering
In the best of human powers:
Ere the fond delusions tire,
Ere envenomed passion grows
From the root of vain desire,—
Mind of Wisdom! interpose!

Now no more in tuneful motion
Life with love and duty glides ;
Reason's meteor-lighted ocean
Bears us down its mazy tides ;
Head is clear and hand is strong,
But our heart no haven knows ;
Sun of Truth ! the night is long,—
Let thy radiance interpose !

―――――

GHOSTS.

WHY wilt Thou ever thus before me stand,
    Thou ghostly Past ?
Always between me and the happy land
    Thy shade is cast.

Thou art no midnight phantom of remorse,
    That I would lay :—
My life has run a plain unnoted course,
    In open day.

I would enjoy the Present, I would live
    Like one new-born :
I value not the gifts Thou hast to give—
    Knowledge and Scorn.

I would, for some short moments, cease to judge—
    Reckon—compare :
And this small bliss Thou wilt persist to grudge,
    Still haunting there.

Thou makest all things heavy with regrets ;
  Too late—too soon :
My mind is like a sun that ever sets,
  And knows no noon :

I am become the very fool of time,—
  The world for me
Has no sure test of innocence or crime ;
  All things may be :

For every notion that has filled my brain
  Leaves such a trace
That every instant it may rise again
  And claim its place.

Faces and fancies I have cursed or cherished
  Throng round my head ;
In vain I call on thee to leave the perished—
  To hide the dead.

Confused and tossed on this ideal sea,
  I hardly keep
A sense of weak and maimed identity,
  More than in sleep :

Save when the Future wins my yearning gaze,
  That shore where still
Imagination resolutely stays
  The tide of ill.

SHADOWS.

I.

THEY owned their passion without shame or fear,
And every household duty counted less
Than that one spiritual bond, and men severe
Said they should sorrow for their wilfulness.

And truth the world went ill with them : he knew
That he had broken up her maiden life,
Where only pleasures and affections grew,
And sowed it thick with labour, pain, and strife.

What her unpractised weakness was to her
The presence of her suffering was to him ;
Thus at Love's feast did Misery minister,
And fill their cups together to the brim.

They asked their kind for hope, but there was none,
Till Death came by and gave them that and more ;
Then men lamented,—but the earth rolls on,
And lovers love and perish as before.

II.

They seemed to those who saw them meet
The worldly friends of every day,
Her smile was undisturbed and sweet,
His courtesy was free and gay.

But yet if one the other's name
In some unguarded moment heard,
The heart, you thought so calm and tame,
Would struggle like a captured bird :

And letters of mere formal phrase
Were blistered with repeated tears,—
And this was not the work of days,
But had gone on for years and years !

Alas, that Love was not too strong
For maiden shame and manly pride !
Alas, that they delayed so long
The goal of mutual bliss beside.

Yet what no chance could then reveal,
And neither would be first to own,
Let fate and courage now conceal,
When truth could bring remorse alone.

III.

Beneath an Indian palm a girl
Of other blood reposes,
Her cheek is clear and pale as pearl,
Amid that wild of roses.

Beside a northern pine a boy
Is leaning fancy-bound,
Nor listens where with noisy joy
Awaits the impatient hound.

Cool grows the sick and feverish calm,—
Relaxed the frosty twine,—
The pine-tree dreameth of the palm,
The palm-tree of the pine.

As soon shall nature interlace
Those dimly-visioned boughs,
As these young lovers face to face
Renew their early vows !

IV.

She had left all on earth for him,
Her home of wealth, her name of pride,
And now his lamp of love was dim,
And, sad to tell, she had not died.

She watched the crimson sun's decline,
From some lone rock that fronts the sea,—
" I would, O burning heart of mine,
There were an ocean-rest for thee.

"The thoughtful moon awaits her turn,
The stars compose their choral crown,
But those soft lights can never burn,
Till once the fiery sun is down."

V.

I had a home wherein the weariest feet
    Found sure repose ;
And Hope led on laborious day to meet
    Delightful close !

A cottage with broad eaves and a thick vine,
    A crystal stream,
Whose mountain-language was the same as mine :
    —It was a dream !

I had a home to make the gloomiest heart
    Alight with joy,—
A temple of chaste love, a place apart
    From Time's annoy ;
A moonlight scene of life, where all things rude
    And harsh did seem
With pity rounded and by grace subdued :
    —It was a dream !

MOMENTS.

I LIE in a heavy trance,
With' a world of dream without me,
Shapes of shadow dance,
In wavering bands, about me ;
But, at times, some mystic things
Appear in this phantom lair,
That almost seem to me visitings
Of Truth known elsewhere :
The world is wide,—these things are small,
They may be nothing, but they are All.

A prayer in an hour of pain,
Begun in an undertone,
Then lowered, as it would fain
Be heard by the heart alone ;

A throb, when the soul is entered
By a light that is lit above,
Where the God of Nature has centered
The Beauty of Love.—
The world is wide,—these things are small,
They may be nothing, but they are All.

A look that is telling a tale,
Which looks alone dare tell,—
When' a cheek is no longer pale,
That has caught the glance, as it fell ;
A touch, which seems to unlock
Treasures unknown as yet,
And the bitter-sweet first shock,
One can never forget ;—
The world is wide,—these things are small,
They may be nothing, but they are All.

A sense of an earnest Will
To help the lowly-living,—
And a terrible heart-thrill,
If you' have no power of giving ;
An arm of aid to the weak,
A friendly hand to the friendless,
Kind words, so short to speak,
But whose echo is endless :
The world is wide,—these things are small,
They may be nothing, but they are All.

The moment we think we have learnt
The lore of the all-wise One,
By which we could stand unburnt,
On the ridge of the seething sun :

The moment we grasp at the clue,
Long-lost and strangely riven,
Which guides our soul to the True,
And the Poet to Heaven.
The world is wide,—these things are small,—
If they be nothing, what is there at all ?

THE MEN OF OLD.

I KNOW not that the men of old
Were better than men now,
Of heart more kind, of hand more bold,
Of more ingenuous brow :
I heed not those who pine for force
A ghost of Time to raise,
As if they thus could check the course
Of these appointed days.

Still it is true, and over true,
That I delight to close
This book of life self-wise and new,
And let my thoughts repose
On all that humble happiness,
The world has since foregone,—
The daylight of contentedness
That on those faces shone !

With rights, tho' not too closely scanned,
Enjoyed, as far as known,—
With will by no reverse unmanned,—
With pulse of even tone,—

They from to-day and from to-night
Expected nothing more,
Than yesterday and yesternight
Had proffered them before.

•

To them was life a simple art
Of duties to be done,
A game where each man took his part,
A race where all must run ;
A battle whose great scheme and scope
They little cared to know,
Content, as men at arms, to cope
Each with his fronting foe.

Man *now* his Virtue's diadem
Puts on and proudly wears,
Great thoughts, great feelings, came to them,
Like instincts, unawares :
Blending their souls' sublimest needs
With tasks of every day,
They went about their gravest deeds,
As noble boys at play.—

And what if Nature's fearful wound
They did not probe and bare,
For that their spirits never swooned
To watch the misery there,—
For that their love but flowed more fast,
Their charities more free,
Not conscious what mere drops they cast
Into the evil sea.

E.

A man's best things are nearest him,
Lie close about his feet,
It is the distant and the dim'
That we are sick to greet :
For flowers that grow our hands beneath
We struggle and aspire,—
Our hearts must die, except they breathe
The air of fresh Desire.

Yet, Brothers, who up Reason's hill
Advance with hopeful cheer,—
O ! loiter not, those heights are chill,
As chill as they are clear ;
And still restrain your haughty gaze,
The loftier that ye go,
Remembering distance leaves a haze
On all that lies below.

———

THE VOICES OF HISTORY.

THE Poet in his vigil hears
Time flowing through the night,—
A mighty stream, absorbing tears,
And bearing down delight :
There resting on his bank of thought
He listens, till his soul
The Voices of the waves has caught,—
The meaning of their roll.

First, wild and wildering as the strife
Of earthly winds and seas,
Resounds the long historic life
Of warring dynasties :—
Uncertain right and certain wrong
In onward conflict driven,
The threats and tramplings of the strong
Beneath a brazen heaven.

The cavernous unsounded East
Outpours an evil tide,
Drowning the hymn of patriarch priest,
The chant of shepherd bride :
How can we catch the angel-word,
How mark the prophet-sound,
'Mid thunders like Niagara's heard
An hundred miles around ?

From two small springs that rise and blend,
And leave their Latin home,
The waters East and West extend,—
The ocean-power of Rome :
Voices of Victories ever-won,
Of Pride that will not stay,
Billows that burst and perish on
The shores that wear away.

Till, in a race of fierce delight
Tumultuous battle forth,
The snows amassed on many a height,
The cataracts of the North :

What can we hear beside the roar,
What see beneath the foam,
What but the wrecks that strew the shore,
And cries of falling Rome ?

Nor, when a purer Faith had traced
Safe channels for the tide,
Did streams with Eden-lilies graced
In Eden-sweetness glide ;
While the deluded gaze admires
The smooth and shining flow,
Vile interests and insane desires
Gurgle and rage below.

If History has no other sounds,
Why should we listen more ?
Spirit ! despise terrestrial bounds,
And seek a happier shore ;
Yet pause ! for on thine inner ear
A mystic music grows,—
And mortal man shall never hear
That diapason's close.

Nature awakes ! a rapturous tone,
Still different, still the same,—
Eternal effluence from the throne
Of Him without a name ;
A symphony of worlds begun,
Ere sin the glory mars,
The cymbals of the new-born sun,
The trumpets of the stars.

Then Beauty all her subtlest chords
Dissolves and knits again,
And Law composes jarring words
In one harmonious chain :
And Loyalty's enchanting notes
Outswelling fade away,
While Knowledge, from ten thousand throats,
Proclaims a graver sway.—

Well, if, by senses unbefooled,
Attentive souls may scan
These great Ideas that have ruled
The total mind of man ;
Yet is there music deeper still,
Of fine and holy woof,
Comfort and joy to all that will
Keep ruder noise aloof.

A music simple as the sky,
Monoto'nous as the sea,
Recurrent as the flowers that die
And rise again in glee :
A melody that childhood sings
Without a thought of art,
Drawn from a few familiar strings,
The fibres of the Heart.

Through tent and cot and proud saloon,
This audible delight
Of nightingales that love the noon,
Of larks that court the night,—

We feel it all,—the hopes and fears
That language faintly tells,
The spreading smiles,—the passing tears,—
The meetings and farewells.

These harmonies that all can share,
When chronicled by one,
Enclose us like the living air,
Unending, unbegun ;—
Poet ! esteem thy noble part,
Still listen, still record,
Sacred Historian of the heart,
And moral nature's Lord !

THE BARREN HILL.

BEFORE my Home, a long straight Hill
   Extends its barren bound,
And all who that way travel will
   Must travel miles around ;
Yet not the loveliest face of earth
   To living man can be
A treasury of more precious worth
   Than that bare Hill to me.

That Hill-side rose a wall between
   This world of ears and eyes
And every shining shifty scene
   That fancy forms and dyes:

First Babyhood engaged its use,
   To plant a good-child's land,
Where all the streams were orange-juice,
   And sugar all the sand.

A playground of unending sward
   There blest the growing Boy,
A dream of labourless reward,
   Whole holidays of joy ;
A book of Nature, whose bright leaves
   No other care should need
Than life that happily receives
   What he that runs may read.

Nor lacked there skies for onward youth
   With wayward will to tinge,
Sweet sunshine overcast by ruth,
   And storms of golden fringe ;
Nor vales that darkling might evoke
   Mysterious fellowship
Of names that still to Fancy woke,
   But slumbered on the lip.

The hour when first that hill I crost,
   Can yet my memory sting,
The dear self-trust that moment lost
   No lore again can bring :
It seemed a foully broken bond
   Of Nature and my kind,
That I should find the world beyond
   The world I left behind.

But not in vain that hill-side stood,
  On many an after-day,
When with returning steps I wooed
  Revival of its sway ;
It could not give me Truth where doubt
  And sin had ample range,
But It was powerful to shut out
  The ill it could not change.

And still performs a sacred part,
  To my experienced eye,
This Pisgah which my virgin heart
  Ascended but to die ;
What was Reality before
  In symbol now may live,
Endowed with right to promise more
  Than ever it could give.

———

THE CHRONICLE OF HOPES.

I WOULD not chronicle my life
By dynasties of joy or pain,
By reigns of peace or times of strife,
By accidents of loss or gain :
The Hopes that nurtured in my breast
Have been the very wings to me
On which existence floats or rests,—
These only shall my eras be.

Whether they rose to utmost height
And glistened in the noonday sun,
Descending with as full delight
When all was realised and won ;
Or whether, mercilessly checked
By adverse airs and lowering skies,
They sunk to earth confused and wrecked
Almost before they dared to rise ;

With equal love I love them all
For their own special sakes, nor care
What sequence here or there might fall,
Each has its sweet memorial share :
Let but my Hopes, in coming years,
Preserve their long unbroken line,
And smiles will shine through any tears,
And grief itself be half-divine.

For not to man on earth is given
The ripe fulfilment of desire ;—
Desire of Heaven itself is Heaven,
Unless the passion faint and tire :
So upward still, from hope to hope,
From faith to faith, the soul ascends,
And who has scaled the ethereal cope,
Where that sublime succession ends ?

THE WORTH OF HOURS.

BELIEVE not that your inner eye
Can ever in just measure try
The worth of Hours as they go by.

For every man's weak self, alas !
Makes him to see them, while they pass,
As through a dim or tinted glass :

But if in earnest care you would
Mete out to each its part of good,
Trust rather to your after-mood.

Those surely are not fairly spent,
That leave your spirit bowed and bent
In sad unrest and ill-content :

And more,—though free from seeming harm.
You rest from toil of mind or arm,
Or slow retire from Pleasure's charm,—

If then a painful sense comes on
Of something wholly lost and gone,
Vainly enjoyed, or vainly done,—

Of something from your being's chain
Broke off, nor to be linked again
By all mere Memory can retain,—

Upon your heart this truth may rise,—
Nothing that altogether dies
Suffices man's just destinies :

So should we live, that every Hour
May die as dies the natural flower,—
A self-reviving thing of power ;

That every Thought and every Deed
May hold within itself the seed
Of future good and future meed ;

Esteeming Sorrow, whose employ
Is to develope not destroy,
Far better than a barren Joy.

HAPPINESS.

I.

BECAUSE the Few with signal virtue crowned,
The heights and pinnacles of human mind,
Sadder and wearier than the rest are found,
Wish not thy Soul less wise or less refined.
True that the small delights which every day
Cheer and distract the pilgrim are not theirs ;
True that, though free from Passion's lawless sway,
A loftier being brings severer cares.
Yet have they special pleasures, even mirth,
By those undreamt-of who have only trod
Life's valley smooth ; and if the rolling earth
To their nice ear have many a painful tone,
They know, Man does not live by Joy alone,
But by the presence of the power of God.

II.

A SPLENDOUR amid glooms,—a sunny thread
Woven into a tapestry of cloud,—
A merry child a-playing with the shroud
That lies upon a breathless mother's bed,—
A garland on the front of one new-wed,
Trembling and weeping while her troth is vowed,—
A school-boy's laugh that rises light and loud
In licensed freedom from ungentle dread ;
These are ensamples of the Happiness,
For which our nature fits us ; more and less
Are parts of all things to the Mortal given,
Of Love, Joy, Truth, and Beauty.   Perfect Light
Would dazzle, not illuminate, our sight,—
From Earth it is enough to glimpse at Heaven.

THE SPRING AND THE BROOK.

IT may be that the Poet is as a Spring,
That, from the deep of being, pulsing forth,
Proffers the hot and thirsty sons of earth
Refreshment unbestowed by sage or king.
Still is he but an utte'rance,—a lone thing,—
Sad-hearted in his very voice of mirth,—
Too often shivering in the thankless dearth
Of those affections he the best can sing.
But Thou, O lively Brook ! whose fruitful way
Brings with it mirror'd smiles, and green, and flowers,—
Child of all scenes, companion of all hours,
Taking the simple cheer of every day,—
How little is to thee, thou happy Mind,
That solitary parent Spring behind !

LOVE WITHOUT SYMPATHY.

YES, I will blame thy very height of heart,
I will conjure thee to remember still
That things above us are not less apart,
And mountains nearest to the sun most chill!
Well hadst thou held sublime and separate rank,
Martyr or heroine of romantic times,
When Woman's life was one poor cloudy blank,
Lit by rare-gleaming virtues, loves, and crimes.
But now that every day for thee and me
Has its own being of delight and woe,
Come down, bright Star! from thy perennial vault,
My earthly path's companion-light to be ;
And I will love thee more for every fault
Than for perfections that the angels show.

———

ON COWPER'S GARDEN AT OLNEY.

FROM this forlornest place, at morn and even,
Issues a voice imperative, "Begone!
All ye that let your vermin thoughts creep on
Beneath the' unheeded thunders of high Heaven ;
Nor welcome they, who, when free grace is given
To flee from usual life's dominion,
Soon as the moving scene or time is gone,
Return, like penitents unfitly shriven.
But Ye, who long have wooed the memory
Of this great Victim of sublime despair,
Encompassed round with evil as with air,
Yet crying, 'God is good, and sinful He,'—
Remain, and feel how better 'tis to drink
Of Truth to Madness ev'en, than shun that fountain's brink."

ON REVISITING TRINITY COLLEGE, CAMBRIDGE.

I HAVE a debt of my heart's own to Thee,
School of my Soul! old lime and cloister shade!
Which I, strange suitor, should lament to see
Fully acquitted and exactly paid.
The first ripe taste of manhood's best delights,
Knowledge imbibed, while mind and heart agree,
In sweet belated talk on winter nights,
With friends whom growing time keeps dear to me,—
Such things I owe thee, and not only these :
I owe thee the far-beaco'ning memories
Of the young dead, who, having crossed the tide
Of Life where it was narrow, deep, and clear,
Now cast their brightness from the further side
On the dark-flowing hours I breast in fear.

GOOD INTENTIONS.

FAIR thoughts of good, and fantasies as fair !
Why is it your content to dwell confined
In the dark cave of meditative mind,
Nor show your forms and colours otherwhere ?
Why taste ye not the beautiful free air
Of life and action ?   If the wintry wind
Rages sometimes, must noble growth be pined,
And fresh extrava'gant boughs lopped off by care?
Behold the budding and the flowe'ring flowers,
That die, and in their seed have life anew ;
Oh ! if the promptings of our better hours
With vegetative virtue sprung and grew,
They would fill up the room of living Time,
And leave the world small space to nourish weeds of crime.

GRAVE TEMPERAMENTS.

To live for present life, and feel no crime—
To see in life a merry-morrice craft,
Where he has done the best who most has laughed,
Is Youth's fit heaven, nor thus the less sublime :
But not to all men, in their best of prime,
Is given by Nature this miracu'lous draught
Of inward happiness, which, hourly quaffed,
Seems to the reveller deep beyond all time.
Therefore encumber not the sad young heart
With exhortations to impossible joy,
And charges of morose and thankless mood ;
For there is working in that Girl or Boy
A power which will and must remain apart—
Only by Love approached and understood.

ACTION AND THOUGHT.

THERE is a world where struggle and stern toil
Are all the nurture of the soul of man—
Ordain'd to raise, from life's ungrateful soil,
Pain as he must, and Pleasure as he can.
Then to that other world of thought from this
Turns the sad soul, all hopeful of repose,
But round in weirdest metamorphosis,
False shapes and true, divine and devilish, close.
Above these two, and resting upon each
A meditative and compassionate eye,
Broodeth the Spirit of God : thence evermore,
On those poor wanderers cast from shore to shore,
Falleth a voice, omnipotent to teach
Them that will hear,—" Despair not ! it is I."

ANIMA MUNDI.

" ANIMA MUNDI "—of thyself existing,
Without diversity or change to fear,
Say, has this Life to which we cling persisting,
Part or communion with thy steadfast sphere?
Does thy serene eternity sublime
Embrace the slaves of Circumstance and Time?

Could we remain continually content
To heap fresh pleasure on the coming day,
Could we rest happy in the sole intent
To make the hours more graceful or more gay ;
Then must the essence of our nature be
That of the beasts that perish, not of Thee.

But if we mourn, not because time is fleeting,
Not because life is short and some die young,
But because parting ever follows meeting,
And, while our hearts with constant loss are wrung,
Our minds are tossed in doubt from sea to sea,
Then may we claim community with thee.

We cannot live by instincts—forced to let
To-morrow's wave obliterate our to-day—
See faces only once—read and forget—
Behold Truth's rays prismatically play
About our mortal eye, and never shine
In one white daylight, simple and divine,

We would erect some Thought the world above,
And dwell in it for ever—we would make
Some moment of young Friendship or First-love
Into a dream, from which we would not wake ;
We would contrast our Action with Repose,
Like the deep stream that widens as it flows.

We would, indeed, be somewise as Thou art,
Not spring and bud and flower and fade and fall,—
Not fix our intellects on some scant part
Of Nature, but enjoy or feel it all:
We would assert the privilege of a soul,
In that it knows—to understand the Whole.

If such things are within us—God is good—
And flight is destined for the callow wing,
And the high appetite implies the food,
And souls must reach the level whence they spring ;
O Life of very Life ! set free our Powers,
Hasten the travail of the yearning hours.

Thou ! to whom old Philosophy bent low,
To the wise few mysteriously revealed ;
Thou ! whom each humble Christian worships now,
In the poor hamlet and the open field ;
Once an Idea—now Comforter and Friend,
Hope of the human Heart ! Descend ! Descend !

CARPE DIEM.

Youth, that pursuest with such eager pace
      Thy even way,
Thou pantest on to win a mournful race :
      Then stay ! oh, stay !

Pause and luxuriate in thy sunny plain ;
      Loiter,—enjoy :
Once past, Thou never wilt come back again,
      A second Boy.

The hills of Manhood wear a noble face,
      When seen from far ;
The mist of light from which they take their grace
      Hides what they are.

The dark and weary path those cliffs between
      Thou canst not know,
And how it leads to regions never-green,
      Dead fields of snow.

Pause, while thou mayst, nor deem that fate thy gain
      Which, all too fast,
Will drive thee forth from this delicious plain,
      A Man at last.

THE FLIGHT OF YOUTH.

No, though all the winds that lie
In the circle of the sky
Trace him out, and pray and moan,
Each in its most plaintive tone,—
No, though Earth be split with sighs,
And all the Kings that reign
Over Nature's mysteries
Be our faithfullest allies,—
All—all is vain :
They may follow on his track,
But He never will come back—
Never again !

Youth is gone away,
Cruel, cruel Youth,
Full of gentleness and ruth
Did we think him all his stay ;
How had He the heart to wreak
Such a woe on us so weak,
He that was so tender-meek ?
How could He be made to learn
To find pleasure in our pain ?
Could he leave us, to return
Never again !

Bow your heads very low,
Solemn-measured be your paces,
Gathered up in grief your faces,
Sing sad music as ye go ;

F 2

In disordered handfuls strew
Strips of cypress, sprigs of rue ;
In your hands be borne the bloom,
Whose long petals once and only
Look from their pink-leavèd tomb
In the midnight lonely ;
Let the nightshade's beaded coral
Fall in melancholy moral
Your wan brows around,
While in very scorn ye fling
The amaranth upon the ground
As an unbelievèd thing ;
What care we for its fair tale
Of beauties that can never fail,
Glories that can never wane ?
No such blooms are on the track
He has past, who will come back
Never again !

Alas ! we know not how He went,
We knew not he was going,
For had our tears once found a vent,
We' had stayed him with their flowing.
It was as an earthquake, when
We awoke and found him gone,
We were miserable men,
We were hopeless, every one !
Yes, He must have gone away
In his guise of every day,
In his common dress, the same
Perfect face and perfect frame ;
For in feature, for in limb,
Who could be compared to him ?

Firm his step, as one who knows
He is free, where'er he goes,
And withal as light of spring
As the arrow from the string :
His impassioned eye had got
Fire which the sun has not ;
Silk to feel, and gold to see,
Fell his tresses full and free,
Like the morning mists that glide
Soft adown the mountain's side ;
Most delicious 'twas to hear
When his voice was trilling clear
As a silver-hearted bell,
Or to follow its low swell,
When, as dreamy winds that stray
Fainting 'mid Æolian chords,
Inner music seemed to play
Symphony to all his words ;
In his hand was poised a spear,
Deftly poised, as to appear
Resting of its proper will,—
Thus a merry hunter still,
And engarlanded with bay,
Must our Youth have gone away,
Though we half remember now,
He had borne some little while
Something mournful in his smile—
Something serious on his brow :
Gentle Heart, perhaps he knew
The cruel deed he was about to do !

Now, between us all and Him
There are rising mountains dim,

Forests of uncounted trees,
Spaces of unmeasured seas :
Think with Him how gay of yore
We made sunshine out of shade,—
Think with Him how light we bore
All the burden sorrow laid ;
All went happily about him,—
How shall we toil on without him?
How without his cheering eye
Constant strength embreathing ever?
How without him standing by
Aiding every hard endeavour?
For when faintness or disease
Had usurped upon our knees,
If He deigned our lips to kiss
With those living lips of his,
We were lightened of our pain,
We were up and hale again :—
Now, without one blessing glance
From his rose-lit countenance,
We shall die, deserted men,—
And not see him, even then !

We are cold, very cold,—
All our blood is drying old,
And a terrible heart-dearth
Reigns for us in heaven and earth :
Forth we stretch our chilly fingers
In poor effort to attain
Tepid embers, where still lingers
Some preserving warmth, in vain.
Oh ! if Love, the Sister dear
Of Youth that we have lost,
Come not in swift pity here,
Come not, with a host

Of Affections, strong and kind,
To hold up our sinking mind,
If She will not, of her grace,
Take her Brother's holy place,
And be to us, at least, a part
Of what He was, in Life and Heart,
The faintness that is on our breath
Can have no other end but Death.

THE WEARY SOUL.

THE Soul is wasted with trouble and toil,
The evening of Life is damp and chill,—
She would go back and rest awhile ;
She can go back whene'er she will,—
For' the Poet holds the Past in fee,
That shadowy land is all his own,
And He, not led by Memory,
But as a man that walks alone
In gardens long familiar, knows
What spots afford the fit repose.

Surely she will not wander far,—
Twilight is coming with never a star ;
Why may she not return where stands,
Broadly towards the westering sun,
That proud building of hearts and hands,
Castle and Palace all in one,
Over the portal named at length,
" Successful Manhood's place of strength ? "
There she may traverse court and hall,
Up to her favourite turret tall ;

She may recline her aching head
On her ancestral purple bed,
There, where at eve so oft she lay,
I' the deep-embrasured window-bay,
Giving her vision open reign
Over the chequered world of plain—
Of hues that rest and hues that pass,
Sunset and autumn and tinted glass;
While the buck's clear bell and the cattle's low,
And every sound that is heard below,
Were melted into one murmur soft
Ere they could reach that couch aloft.

Witness of that triumphant scene !
Little you know what doom has been :—
How at a blow the heavens were split,
Words on the wall spontaneous writ,
As with a pen of burning brass,
" Vanitas, omnia Vanitas : "—
How disappointment bared her hand,
Vivid and red as the levin brand,
Struck on the tower's sublimest crown,
Shattered the sturdiest buttress down,—
Till the poor Soul would fain have died
'Mid her annihilated pride.
Speed her along, tho' night be drear,—
Night be her cover, for none is here ;
Seek her a rest where'er you may,
Not in this shelterless decay !

There is a bower, a way-side bower,
Rich with brede of berry' and flower,—
Fair to dwell in and behold
How the green is turning gold,

Till the leafy screen repeat
All the life without the heat :
Music comes not here and there,
Does not fill, but is, the air :
Perfumes delicate and fine,
Flower of orange, flower of vine,
Take their place, without pretence,
In the harmony of sense ;
Where the floating spirit dreams,
Fed by odours, sounds, and gleams,
Of this royal region hight,
" Youth's dominion of delight."
Why then farther ? why not here ?
Soul of sorrow, Mind of fear !
Rest, as thou wert wont to rest,
On the swell of Nature's breast.
Hear that voice in angel's frame,
Singing, " Youth is still the same ;
Cheery faces glimpsing round,—
Limber feet on mossy ground ;
Circumstance, the God of clay,
We have fairly laughed away,
And a power of other face,
Hope, is seated in his place.
Enter, all that come from far,
Poor and naked as ye are ;
Very breath is here divine,—
Bacchus has no need of wine !"

" Friends !" the tearful soul replies,
" Keep, oh ! keep your Paradise !
Once I gained your happy place,
Ardent in the healthy race,

One of many braced together,
Comrades of the way and weather;
Now alone I falter by,—
Youth's the same,—but what am I?
Just as sweet, as free from cares,
Are your smiles,—but are not *theirs:*
When the lips I pressed of old
Lie beneath the sullen mould:
When the voices I have known
In hosannas like your own
Answer to my yearning call,
Thin and feeble, if at all;
When the golden locks are grey,
That made sunshine all my day;
When my fibres fall together
In your genial summer-weather;—
How can I repose an hour
In the graces of your bower?
How should I take up my rest,
As a strange unnatural guest,
In this home of truth, in this
My retreat of ancient bliss?
Blasts of death-impregnate air
Would, with all the flowers, be there,—
Storms thro' all the blue be spread
In thick battalia o'er my head;
Pallid looks of friendships broken,
Phantom words unwisely spoken,
Thoughts of love and self-reproof
Mingled in a fearful woof,—
Wishes, when not wished in vain,
Only realised for pain,—
Things ye could not hear or see
Would be all my company!"

Disheartened spirit! thou art then
In vain distinct from common men,
If all thy weary quest of mind
No true abiding-place can find,
Whose charms the busy life subdue,
And lure it from the outer view!
No region of thy mortal lot
Where Peace is native to the spot,
Ready to greet, when care-begone,
Imagination's pilgrim son.

Yet onward;—it is well to stray
Along this bleak and homeless way,
Till thou canst raise thy conscious eyes
Where Childhood's Atalantis lies,
And recognise that idyl scene,
Where all mild creatures, void of awe,
Amid field-flowers and mountains green,
Fulfil their being's gentle law.

They will not fear thee; safe they dwell
Within this armless citadel,
Embastioned in the self-defence
Of self-regardless innocence:
On Sin or Sorrow's bosom lingers
Each infant head in slumbers bland,—
Secure the tender tiny fingers
Enclasp the dark and withered hand.

Abysms of thought and sense must be
Between those simple souls and thee;
But as the parent is beguiled
Into the nature of the child,

So mayst thou, tho' an alien here,
By careful duty take thy part
In all the feelings that endear
The kingdom of the virgin heart.

And thou wilt taste once more the rills
Fresh gushing from the eternal hills,
And feel delight in living air
Without research of when and where ;
And hear the birds their song dispense
With free descant, on branch and wing,
Careless of other audience
Than God who made and bade them sing.

Till haply pausing some noon-day
Amid the fairy-people's play,
Along thy limbs the stony sleep
That rounds our life shall calmly creep,
And thou from Present and from Past,
And things to come at once be freed,
To rest for aye, or wake at last
In God's own arms, a child indeed.

THE WORLD TO THE SOUL.

SOUL ! that may'st have been divine,
Now I claim and take thee mine ;
Now thy mortal bliss must be
In thy loyalty to me.

Though thou seemest without stain,
There is evil in thy grain ;
Thou hast tasted of the fruit
Of which Knowledge is the root.

So I must not let thee rest,
Lull'd on Faith's maternal breast ;
Faith and Fancy mar the plan
Of the making of a man.

So thy tender heart I bare
To Ambition's frosty air ;
So I plunge thee deep in doubt,
That thou may'st grow hard and stout.

So I bid the eager Boy
Sense in every form enjoy ;
Stinting not the moment's pleasure,
Save to gain some fuller measure.

Thou wilt lose at last the zest,
Thou wilt need some higher quest ;
Then I bid thee rise a Man,
And I aid thee all I can.

Fix thee on some worthy aim,
Proving danger, fronting shame ;
Knowing only friends or foes,
As they speed thee or oppose :

Trampling with thy rapid feet
Feelings fond and pleas discreet ;
Only for excuses sue
In the great things thou canst do.

If what shone afar so grand,
Turn to nothing in thy hand,
On, again—the virtue lies
In the struggle, not the prize ;

Only rest not : failure-curst
Turn to Pleasure at the worst ;
That may calm thy conscience-cry—
Death may give thee peace, not I.

———

THE PALSY OF THE HEART.

I SEE the worlds of earth and sky
  With beauty filled to overflow ;
My spirit lags behind the eye—
  I know, but feel not as I know :
Those miracles of form and hue
  I can dissect with artist skill,
But more than this I cannot do,—
  Enjoyment rests beyond the will.

Round me in rich profusion lie
  Nectareous fruits of ancient mind,
The thoughts that have no power to die
  In golden poesy enshrined :
And near me hang, of later birth,
  Ripe clusters from the living tree,
But what the pleasure, what the worth,
  If all is savourless to me !

I hear the subtle chords of sound,
    Entangled, loosed, and knit anew ;
The music floats without—around—
    But will not enter and imbue :
While harmonies diviner still,
    Sweet greetings, appellations dear,
That used through every nerve to thrill
    I often hear, and only hear.

O dreadful thought ! if by God's grace
    To souls like mine there should be given
That perfect presence of his face,
    Which we, for want of words, call Heaven,—
And unresponsive even there
    This heart of mine could still remain,
And its intrinsic evil bear
    To realms that know no other pain.

Better down nature's scale to roll,
    Far as the base unbreathing clod,
Than rest a conscious reasoning soul,
    Impervious to the light of God ;—
Hateful the powers that but divine
    What we have lost beyond recal,
The intellectual plummet-line
    That sounds the depths to which we fall.

THE MARTYRS OF THE MIND.

HONOUR to the sacred Past !
    Reverence to the ancient days !
Yet believe them not the last
    That demand your love and praise :

Think not that the olden story
  Can within its depth enfold
All the beauty and the glory
  That the heart of Man can hold.

Think not rashly that, because
  Modern life is smooth and fine,
'Tis not subject to the laws
  Of the Master's high design :
That we less require endurance
  Than in days of coarser plan,—
That we less demand assurance
  Of the Godhead hid in Man.

Trust me, Truth is still at war,
  Just as in the hard old time,
With a thousand things that are—
  Births of woe and food for crime :
Still to vindicate the right
  Is a rough and thankless game ;
Still the leader in the fight
  Is the hindmost in the fame.

True, the penal fires are out—
  True, the rack in rust has lain—
But the secret burning Doubt
  And the pangs of Thought remain :
True, the mind of Man is free—
  Free to speak and write at will,
But a power you cannot see
  Still can plague, and waste, and kill.

Very tame our passions nestle,
  Very even seem our brows,
Outward forces rarely wrestle,
  Soft the words the age allows :
Incommunicable sadness
  Yet is haunting all the while—
Yet one day the crouching madness
  Leaps from under all the smile.

Ours is not the early Faith
  Which our fathers gazed upon,
Till the iron gates of Death
  With a golden splendour shone ;
We must rest content with Hope,
  Fair to aid, but frail to rule :
Gentle Hope ! too weak to cope
  With the villain and the fool.

Ours the shame to understand
  That the World prefers the lie
That, with medicine in her hand,
  She *will* sink and choose to die ;
Ours the agonising sense
  Of the Heaven this Earth might be,
If, from their blank indifference,
  Men woke one hour and felt as we !

Heroes of the inward strife,
  Whom your spirit cannot prize ;
Saints of the mysterious life,
  Whom no Church can canonize ;

G

Unremembered—unrecorded—
  They are passing by you now ;
Other gifts are here rewarded,
  To far other names you bow.

Yet the Power appears to-morrow,
  That to-day seems wholly lost,
And the reproductive sorrow
  Is a treasure worth the cost :
Fate permits no break or suture
  In the' Ideal of Mankind,
Weaving out its brightest Future
  From the Martyrs of the Mind.

WRITTEN FOR THE CONSUMPTIVE HOSPITAL.

If parting hours are ever had
  In reverence among men ;
If fierce emotions turn to sad,
  And sins to sorrows then ;
If the grave presence of the Last
  The lightest scenes can hallow,
Adorn each desert of the Past,
  And deepen every shallow :

Then, surely, in the hours that rend
  The spirit from the frame
In which it dwelt so long, and send
  The dust to whence it came ;

'Tis, above all things, well that those
   About to go for ever,
Should solemnly and calmly close
   Their scene of hard Endeavour !

Gladly the soldier falls in strife
   Hailed by his comrades' cheers ;
Bravely the wise man yields his life
   Amid familiar tears ;
But rare must be his spirit's tone,
   Who, after years repented,
Can dare lie down and die alone,
   Neglected, unlamented !

Through Faith the yearning eye may fix
   On joys that almost blind,
Yet should some gentle feelings mix,
   For what is left behind.
And, if both heart and mind grow weak
   In agony or languor,
Let the last wandering accents speak
   Of sorrow, not of anger !

Oh ! who can tell how far may fly
   Into the world unseen,
The record of some pitying sigh,
   Some sympathetic mien :
How deep may the abyss be stirred
   Of ghostly recollection !
How long may last one casual word
   Of brotherly affection !

Then aid our work ; help us who strive
    To check the' insidious ill
That gives to death those most alive,
    And beautifies to kill ;
Help us who, at the worst, can sooth
    The heart's last fatal swelling,
The' inevitable bed can smooth,
    And light the narrow dwelling.

While Fortune's favours round you smile,
    'Tis something, even then,
To know you helped to reconcile
    A man with brother men ;
And when, through waves that round you roll,
    Your heart is hardly faring,
'Tis more to think you saved one soul
    From dying God-despairing !

SECOND CHILDHOOD.

TAKE not Childhood's name in vain,
Give it not to Him :
Can the lees of life retain
Bubbles from the brim ?
What can Childhood—made to deck
Time with early flowers—
Have in common with the wreck
Of uncounted hours ?

Nothing but the ignorance—
Not of things unknown—
But forgotten, like a glance,
Vanished, like a tone !
Nothing but the froward will,
Now without controul,
Self-absorbed, for good or ill
Of body and of soul.

Childhood without dignity,—
Childhood without grace,—
Childhood with the sunken eye
And the wasted face :
Childhood, vain of petty skill,
Proud of little lore,
Yet devoid of power or will
To advance to more.

Oh ! that each of us might die
When we're at the best !
Pass away harmoniously
To some fitting rest !
No travestied childhood then
Could abuse the word,—
Each would say, a man to men,
" I go—so wills the Lord."

Then the Few whose age endured
With untarnished worth,
Would go down with fame assured,
Moral kings of earth :

Then such memo'ries as the young
Now can only claim,
Would entrance the loving tongue
With the honoured name.

Then nor Love nor Life would pall,
Ere its work was done :
Honest tears would freely fall—
Tears that injure none.
Sad indeed to close dear eyes
That shall gaze no more ;
How much sadder to despise
Those revered before !

Think not that the world would lose
By the' arrested heart ;
All men, at some moment, choose
The diviner part :
Happy then to close their lot
Wheresoever found,
Garnered up, nor left to rot
On the' ungenial ground.

THE OLD MAN'S SONG.

AGE is not a thing to measure
By the course of moon or star ;
Time's before us ; at our pleasure
We may follow near or far :

Strength and Beauty he has given—
They are his to take away ;
But the Heart that well has striven
Is no slave of Night or Day.

See, upon yon mountain-ridges,
How the fir-woods spread between,
Reconcile the snow-clad edges
With the valley's vernal green :
So the lines of grave reflection,
You decipher on my brow,
Keep my age in glad connexion
With the young that flourish now.

Not that now poetic fire
Can along my life-strings run,
As when my Memnonian lyre
Welcomed every rising sun ;
Though my heart no more rejoices
In the flashes of my brain,
In the freshness of *your* voices
Let me hear my songs again.

Did I love ?—let Nature witness,
Conscious of my tears and truth ;
Do I love ?—O fatal fitness !
Still requiring youth for youth !
Yet, while thought the bliss remembers,
All delight is not gone by ;
Warm your spirits o'er my embers,
Friends ! and learn to love as I.

O my children ! O my brothers !
If for self I lived too much,
Be my pleasures now for others,
Every passion now be such :
Be the chillness life-destroying,
That could make me slow to feel,
To enjoy with your enjoying,
To be zealous with your zeal.

Grant me not, ye reigning Hours !
Virtues that beseem the young,
Vigour for my failing powers,
Music for my faltering tongue :
Let me, cheerful thoughts retaining,
Live awhile, nor fear to die,
Ever new affections gaining,
Such as Heaven might well supply.

JUNE, 1843.

DOMESTIC FAME.

WHY is the Grave so silent ?   Why is the Tomb so dead?
Wherefore this gloomy secret on each departed head ?

Why do we name them seldom, and then with voices low,
As if some shame were on them, or superhuman woe ?

Were Death the sleep eternal that some despairing feign,
Had never Faith engendered the hope to meet again,—

Still why should this great absence obliterate with its tears
The happiest recollections and sympathies of years ?

Oh, no ! Death could not banish the love that lived complete,
And passed away untarnished to its celestial seat !

Oh, no ! 'tis not the living that we should harshly blame,
But that men lightly cherish their pure domestic fame.

How few leave not behind them some cause to bless the tomb,
That mercifully closes, and pardons in its gloom !

How few go from us, leaving the thoughts of them so dear,
That aye the prayer besets us, " O God ! that they were here ! "

So that in distant evenings, when joyous faces glow
About the Christmas fire-light and laughter melts the snow,—

In pauses of the revel, some heart without a fear,
Will passionately murmur—" Ah ! why are they not here ? "

Or that in weary seasons, when sickness racks the brain,
And lordly Reason falters, and Will is only pain,—

Those whom they loved to counsel may mystically hear
Their voices leading onwards the path they trod when here :

Or that in awful moments, when evil seems set free
To tempt mankind to question what God of Truth there be,—

The sense how *they*, too, suffered and conquered, serves to cheer
The struggler, dimly conscious of spirits watching near.

Not, then, to Heroes only, to Poet, Statesman, King,
Let care of future glory its anxious duties bring ;

There is no name so lowly, that may not raise a shrine
Of living hearts, to honour its memory as Divine !

IN MEMORIAM.

MRS. EDWARD DENISON.

'Tis right for her to sleep between
  Some of those old Cathedral walls,
And right too that her grave is green
  With all the dew and rain that falls.

'Tis well the organ's solemn sighs
  Should soar and sink around her rest,
And almost in her ear should rise
  The prayers of those she loved the best.

'Tis also well this air is stirred
  By Nature's voices loud and low,
By thunder and the chirping bird,
  And grasses whispering as they grow.

For all her spirit's earthly course
  Was as a lesson and a sign
How to o'errule the hard divorce
  That parts things natu'ral and divine.

Undaunted by the clouds of fear,
  Undazzled by a happy day,
She made a Heaven about her here,
  And took how much ! with her away.

SALISBURY, Nov. 1843.

MARY AND AGNES BERRY.

November 27, 1852.

Two friends within one grave we place,
   United in our tears,
Sisters, scarce parted for the space
   Of more than eighty years :
And she, whose bier is borne to-day,
   The one the last to go,
Bears with her thoughts that force their way
   Above the moment's woe :

Thoughts of the varied human life
   Spread o'er that field of time—
The toil, the passion, and the strife,
   The virtue and the crime :
Yet 'mid this long tumultuous scene,
   The image on our mind
Of these dear women rests serene
   In happy bounds confined.

Within one undisturbed abode
   Their presence seems to dwell,
From which continual pleasures flowed,
   And countless graces fell :
Not unbecoming this our age
   Of decorative forms,
Yet simple as the hermitage
   Exposed to Nature's storms.

Our English grandeur on the shelf
　　Deposed its decent gloom,
And every pride unloosed itself
　　Within that modest room ;
Where none were sad and few were dull,
　　And each one said his best,
And beauty was most beautiful,
　　With vanity at rest.

Brightly the day's discourse rolled on,
　　Still casting on the shore
Memorial pearls of times bygone
　　And worthies now no more :
And little tales of long ago
　　Took meaning from those lips,
Wise chroniclers of joy and woe,
　　And eyes without eclipse.

No taunt or scoff obscured the wit
　　That there rejoiced to reign ;
They never would have laughed at it
　　If it had carried pain.
There needless scandal, e'en though true,
　　Provoked no bitter smile,
And even men-of-fashion grew
　　Benignant for awhile.

Not that there lacked the nervous scorn
　　At every public wrong—
Not that a friend was left forlorn
　　When victim of the strong ;

Free words expressing generous blood
  No nice punctilio weighed,
For deep an earnest womanhood
  Their reason underlaid.

As generations onward came
  They loved from all to win
Revival of the sacred flame
  That glowed their hearts within ;
While others in time's greedy mesh
  The faded garlands flung,
Their hearts went out and gathered fresh
  Affections from the young.

Farewell, dear Ladies ! in your loss
  We feel the past recede,
The gap, our hands could almost cross,
  Is now a gulf indeed.
Ye, and the days in which your claims
  And charms were early known,
Lose substance, and ye stand as names
  That history makes its own.

Farewell ! the pleasant social page
  Is read ; but ye remain
Examples of ennobled age,
  Long life without a stain ;
A lesson to be scorned by none,
  Least by the wise and brave,
Delightful as the winter sun
  That gilds this open grave.

LADY CAMPBELL.

GENTLY supported by the ready aid
Of loving hands, whose little work of toil
Her grateful prodigality repaid
With all the benediction of her smile,
She turned her failing feet
To the soft-pillowed seat,
Dispensing kindly greetings all the while.

Before the tranquil beauty of her face
I bowed in spirit, thinking that she were
A suffe'ring Angel, whom the special grace
Of God entrusted to our pious care,
That we might learn from her
The art to minister
To heavenly beings in seraphic air.

There seemed to lie a weight upon her brain,
That ever pressed her blue-veined eyelids down,
But could not dim her lustrous eyes with pain,
Nor seam her forehead with the faintest frown :
She was as she were proud,
So young, to be allowed
To follow Him who wore the thorny crown.

Nor was she sad, but over every mood,
To which her lightly-pliant mind gave birth,
Gracefully changing, did a spirit brood,
Of quiet gaiety, and serenest mirth ;

And thus her voice did flow,
So beautifully low,
A stream whose music was no thing of earth.

Now long that instrument has ceased to sound,
Now long that gracious form in earth has lain
Tended by nature only, and unwound
Are all those mingled threads of Love and Pain ;
So let me weep and bend
My head and wait the end,
Knowing that God creates not thus in vain.

GEORGE VERNON COLEBROKE.

THOU too art gone, and yet I hardly know
    Why thou didst care to go :
Thou wert so well at heart, so spirit-clear,
    So heavenly-calm, though here ;
But thus it is ; and, it would seem, no more
    Can we, who on the shore
Of the loud world still walk, escape the din,
    And lie awhile within
The quiet sunlight of thy filmless mind
    And rise refreshed, refined ;
Yet am I mild and tempered in my grief,
    Having a sure relief ;—
For these dear hours on life's dull length were sprent,
    By rarest accident,
And *now* I have thee by me when I will,
    Hear thy wise words, and fill
My soul with thy calm looks ; *now* I can tame
    Ill thoughts by thy mere name.

Death, the Divorcer, has united us
  With bands impervious
To any tooth of Time, for they are wove
Of the same texture as an Angel's Love.

FEBRUARY 23, 1835.

        ————

ARTHUR AND ELLEN HALLAM.

A BROTHER and a Sister,—these two Friends,
Cast by fond Nature in one common mould,
And waited on by genial circumstance
In all their history of familiar love,
After a parting of not quite four years,
Are peacefully united here once more.

  He-first, as best beseemed the manly mind,
Tried the dark walk, which has (or seems to have)
No portion in the pleasant sun or stars,
The breath of flowers or morning-song of birds,
The hand of Friendship or the lips of Love.
Whether her sad and separated soul
Received some token from that secret place,
That she might follow him and meet him there,
Or whether God, displeased that anything
Of good or evil should so long divide
Such undefiled and sacred sympathies,
Has made them one again before his face,
Are things that we perhaps shall never know.

  Say not, O world of short and broken sight !
That these died young : the bee and butterfly
Live longer in one active sunny hour

Than the poor tortoise in his torpid years :
The lofty flights of Thought through clear and cloud,—
The labyrinthine ways that Poesy
Leads her beloved, the weary traverses
Of Reason, and the haven of calm Faith,
All had been theirs ; their seamless brows had known
The seal of pain, the sacrament of tears ;
And, unless Pride and Passion and bold Sin
Are all the rule and reckoning of our Being,
They have fulfilled as large a task of life
As ever vete'ran on the mortal field.

Thus they who gave these favoured creatures birth
Deem it no hard infraction of the law
Which regulates the order of our race,
That they above their offspring raise the tomb,
And with parental piety discharge
The duties filial love delights to pay :
They read the perfect sense of the design
In that which seems exception, and they mourn,
Not that these dear ones are already gone,
But that *they* linger still so far behind.

TO A MOURNER.

SLEEP not—you whose hope is dust,
  Love-deserted man !
Or, if feeble body must,
  Seldom as it can.

H

Sleep is kin to Death, they tell,—
You for this might love it well,
But it is a kinsman poor,
Hardly gets beyond the door,—
Never fairly dwells within
  Where they rest and weep not
Who are safe from Pain and Sin ;
  Sleep not, Mourner, sleep not.

Mise'ry spent revives in Sleep,
  Will has no resistance,
Anguish delves abysses deep
  In that dream-existence.
Then we wake and half-believe,
That we may ourselves deceive,
That the loss our souls deplore
May be but a dream the more ;—
Till, at one sharp start, we know,
  Though we shriek and weep not,
Our *reality* of woe,—
  Therefore, brother, sleep not !

But let Sleep some wayward change
  Bring upon our being,
Let sweet fancies freely range
  With calm thoughts agreeing :
Let sad memory be abused
By the pleasure circumfused,
And dear forms no more below
Softly round us come and go ;
Or let time be buried quite,
  And the moments creep not,—
Though oblivion be delight,
  Still, poor mourner, sleep not !

For an Agony will come,
　In the instant waking,
Like a dagger driven home,
　Like a nerve in breaking ;
Consciousness recovering life
But confounds us in the strife,
Wholly yielded up to Pain,
As when drowned men feel again ;
In that rush of gasping thought,
　Wo for them that weep not !
Too, too dearly may be bought
　Such repose—oh ! sleep not !

Rather think the Evil down,
　Rather weep it out ;
Certain grief remits its frown
　Easier than doubt.
There are strong yet gentle powers
In the growth of many hours ;
Sorrow longer-lived will gain
Something more of peace than pain,
Such as God's still works possess,
　Things that sow or reap not
In the world of more and less,
　Live and die, but sleep not.

REQUIESCAT IN PACE.

WE have watched him to the last
We have seen the dreaded king
Smile pacific, as he past
By that couch of suffering :

Wrinkles of aggressive years,
Channels of recondite tears,
Furrows on the anxious brow
All are smooth as childhood's now.—
Death, as seen by men in dreams,
Something stern and cruel seems,
But his face is not the same,
When he comes into the room,
Takes the hand, and names the name,
Seals the eyes with tender gloom,
Saying, "Blessed are the laws
To which all God's creatures bend :
Mortal ! fear me not, because
Thine inevitable friend !"

So when all the limbs were still,
Moved no more by sense or will,
Reve'rent hands the body laid
In the Church's pitying shade,
With the pious rites that fall,
Like the rain-drops, upon all.
What could man refuse or grant
The spiritual inhabitant,
Who so long had ruled within
With power to sin or not to sin ?
Nothing.   Hope, and hope alone,
Mates with death.   Upon a stone
Let the simple name be writ,
Traced upon the infant's front
Years ago : and under it,
As with Christian folk is wont,
"*Requiescat*" or, may be,
Symbol letters, R. I. P.   .

Rest is happy—rest is right,
Rest is precious in God's sight.
But if He, who lies below,
Out of an abundant heart
Drawing remedies for woe,
Never wearied to impart
Blessings to his fellow-men ;
If he never rested then,
But each harvest gathered seed
For the future word and deed,—
And the darkness of his kind
Filled him with such endless ruth,
That the very light of truth
Pained him walking 'mid the blind,—
How, when some transcendant change
Gives his being boundless range,—
When he knows not time or space,
In the nearness of God's face,—
In the world of spirits how
Shall that soul be resting now ?
While one creature is unblest,
How can such as he have rest ?

" Rest in Peace," the legend runs,
Rest is sweet to Adam's sons.
But can he whose busy brain
Worked within this hollow skull,
Now his zeal for truth restrain,
Now his subtle fancy dull,
When he wanders spirit-free
In his young immortality !
While on earth he only bore
Life, as it was linked with lore,

And the infinite increase
Of, knowledge was his only peace ;
Till that knowledge be possest
How can such a mind have rest ?

Rest is happy—rest is meet
For well-worn and weary feet,
Surely not for him, on whom
Ponderous stands the pompous tomb,
Prompt to blind the Future's eyes
With gilt deceit, and blazoned lies :
Him, who never used his powers
To speed for good the waiting hours,
Made none wiser for his seeing,
Made none better for his being ;
Closed his eyes, lest others' woes
Should disturb his base repose ;
Catching at each selfish zest ;
How can he have right to rest ?
Rather we would deem him driven
Anywhere in search of heaven,
Failing ever in the quest,
Till he learns it is not given
That man should by himself be blest.

Here we struggle with the light,
And when comes the fated night,
Into Nature's lap we fall,
Like tired children, one and all.
Day and Labour, Night and Rest,
Come together in our mind,
And we image forth the blest
To eternal calm resigned :

Yet it may be that the' abyss
Of the lost is only this,
That for them all things to come
Are inanimate and dumb,
And immortal life they steep
In dishonourable sleep :
While no power of pause is given
To the inheritors of Heaven ;
And the holiest still are those
Who are furthest from repose,
And yet onward, onward, press
To a loftier godliness ;
Still becoming, more than being,
Apprehending, more than seeing,
Feeling, as from orb to orb
In their awful course they run,
How their souls new light absorb
From the self-existing One,—
Demiurgos, throned above,
Mind of Mind, and Love of Love.

A SONG OF THOUGHTS.

LET the lays from poet-lips
Shadow forth the speech of heaven,—
Let melodious airs eclipse
All delight to senses given ;
Yet to these my notes and words
Listen with your heart alone,
While the Thought that best accords
Makes a music of its own.

Ye that in the fields of Love
Feel the breath and bloom of spring,
While I sing, securely rove,—
Rest in safety, while I sing.
Ye that gaze with vain regret
Back towards that holy ground,
All the world between forget,
Spirit-rocked from sound to sound.

All indifference, all distrust,
From old friendships pass away !
Let the faces of the just
Shine as in God's perfect day !
Fix the faintest, fleetest, smile,
E'er athwart your path has gleam'd,—
Take the charm without the wile,—
Be the Beauty all it seem'd !

'Mid the flowers you love the best,
Summer pride or vernal boon—
By your favou'rite light caressed,
Blush of eve or glow of noon,—
Blend the strains of happiest days
With the voices held most dear ;
Children cast on weary ways !
Rest in peace and pleasaunce here.

Be the Future's glorious page
In my tones to youth revealed ;
Let the ruffled brow of age
With eternal calm be sealed ;

High as Heaven's ethereal cope,
Wide as Light's rejoicing ray,
Thoughts of memory ! Thoughts of hope !
Wander, wander, while ye may.

A CHILD'S SONG.

" I see the Moon, and the Moon sees me,
  God bless the Moon, and God bless me."
                            OLD RHYME.

LADY Moon, Lady Moon, where are you roving ?
        Over the sea.
Lady Moon, Lady Moon, whom are you loving ?
        All that love me.

Are you not tired with rolling, and never
        Resting to sleep ?
Why look so pale, and so sad, as for ever
        Wishing to weep ?

Ask me not this, little child ! if you love me ;
        You are too bold ;
I must obey my dear Father above me,
        And do as I'm told.

Lady Moon, Lady Moon, where are you roving ?
        Over the sea.
Lady Moon, Lady Moon, whom are you loving ?
        All that love me.

GOOD NIGHT AND GOOD MORNING.

(A CHILD'S SONG.)

A FAIR little girl sat under a tree,
Sewing as long as her eyes could see:
Then smoothed her work, and folded it right,
And said, "Dear Work! Good Night, Good Night!"

Such a number of rooks came over her head,
Crying "Caw! caw!" on their way to bed:
She said, as she watched their curious flight,
"Little black things! Good Night! Good Night!"

The horses neighed, and the oxen lowed:
The sheep's "Bleat! bleat!" came over the road:
All seeming to say, with a quiet delight,
"Good little Girl! Good Night! Good Night!"

She did not say to the Sun "Good Night!"
Though she saw him there, like a ball of light;
For she knew he had God's time to keep
All over the world, and never could sleep.

The tall pink foxglove bowed his head—
The violets curtsied and went to bed;
And good little Lucy tied up her hair,
And said, on her knees, her favourite prayer.

And while on her pillow she softly lay
She knew nothing more till again it was day:
And all things said to the beautiful sun,
"Good Morning! Good Morning! our work is begun!"

THE LAY OF THE HUMBLE.

Le bon Dieu me dit—"Chante,
Chante, pauvre petit." BERANGER.

I HAVE no comeliness of frame,
No pleasant range of feature ;
I'm feeble, as when first I came
To earth, a weeping creature ;
My voice is low whene'er I speak,
And singing faint my song ;
But though thus cast among the weak,
I envy not the strong.

The trivial part in life I play
Can have so light a bearing
On other men, who, night or day,
For me are never caring ;
That, though I find not much to bless,
Nor food for exaltation,
I know that I am tempted less,—
And that is consolation.

The beautiful ! the noble blood !
I shrink as they pass by,—
Such power for evil or for good
Is flashing from each eye ;
They are indeed the stewards of Heaven,
High-headed and strong-handed :
From those, to whom so much is given,
How much may be demanded !

'Tis true, I am hard buffeted,
Though few can be my foes,
Harsh words fall heavy on my head,
And unresisted blows ;
But then I think, "had I been born,—
Hot spirit—sturdy frame—
And passion prompt to follow scorn,—
I might have done the same."

To me men are for what they are,
They wear no masks with me ;
I never sicken'd at the jar
Of ill-tuned flattery ;
I never mourned affections lent
In folly or in blindness ;—
The kindness that on me is spent
Is pure, unasking, kindness.

And most of all, I never felt
The agonizing sense
Of seeing love from passion melt
Into indifference ;
The fearful shame, that day by day
Burns onward, still to burn,
To' have thrown your precious heart away,
And met this black return.

I almost fancy that the more
I am cast out from men,
Nature has made me of her store
A worthier denizen ;

As if it pleased her to caress
A plant grown up so wild,
As if the being parentless
Made me the more *her* child.

Athwart my face when blushes pass
To be so poor and weak,
I fall into the dewy grass,
And cool my fevered cheek ;
And hear a music strangely made,
That you have never heard,
A sprite in every rustling blade,
That sings like any bird.

My dreams are dreams of pleasantness,—
But yet I always run,
As to a father's morning kiss,
When rises the round sun ;
I see the flowers on stalk and stem,
Light shrubs, and poplars tall,
Enjoy the breeze,—I rock with them,—
We're merry brothers all.

I do remember well, when first
I saw the great blue sea,—
It was no stranger-face, that burst
In terror upon me ;
My heart began, from the first glance,
His solemn pulse to follow,
I danced with every billow's dance,
And shouted to their hollo.

The Lamb that at its mother's side
Reclines, a tremulous thing,
The Robin in cold winter-tide,
The Linnet in the spring,
All seem to be of kin to me,
And love my slender hand,—
For we are bound, by God's decree,
In one defensive band.

And children, who the worldly mind
And ways have not put on,
Are ever glad in me to find
A blithe companion :
And when for play they leave their homes,
Left to their own sweet glee,
They hear my step, and cry, " He comes,
Our little friend,—'tis he."

Have you been out some starry night,
And found it joy to bend
Your eyes to one particular light,
Till it became a friend ?
And then, so loved that glistening spot,
That, whether it were far
Or more or less, it mattered not,—
It still was your own star.

Thus, and thus only, can you know,
How I, even scornèd I,
Can live in love, tho' set so low,
And' my ladie-love so high ;

Thus learn, that on this varied ball,
Whate'er can breathe and move,
The meanest, lornest, thing of all—
Still owns its right to love.

With no fair round of household cares
Will my lone hearth be blest,
Never the snow of my old hairs
Will touch a loving breast ;
No darling pledge of spousal faith
Shall I be found possessing,
To whom a blessing with my breath
Would be a double blessing :

But yet my love with sweets is rife,
With happiness it teems,
It beautifies my waking life,
And waits upon my dreams ;
A shape that floats upon the night,
Like foam upon the sea,—
A voice of seraphim,—a light
Of present Deity !

I hide me in the dark arcade,
When she walks forth alone,—
I feast upon her hair's rich braid,—
Her half-unclaspèd zone :
I watch the flittings of her dress,
The bending boughs between,—
I trace her footsteps' faery press
On' the scarcely ruffled green.

Oh deep delight! the frail guitar
Trembles beneath her hand,
She sings a song she brought from far,
I cannot understand ;
Her voice is always as from heaven,
But yet I seem to hear
Its music best, when thus 'tis given
All music to my ear.

She' has turned her tender eyes around,
And seen me crouching there,
And smiles, just as that last full sound
Is fainting on the air ;
And now, I can go forth so proud,
And raise my head so tall.—
My heart within me beats so loud,
And musical withal :—

And there is summer all the while,
Mid-winter tho' it be,—
How should the universe not smile,
When she has smiled on me?
For tho' that smile can nothing more
Than merest pity prove,
Yet pity, it was sung of yore,
Is not *so* far from love.

From what a crowd of lovers' woes
My weakness is exempt !
How far more fortunate than those
Who mark me for contempt !

No fear of rival happiness
My fervent glory smothers,
The zephyr fans me none the less
That it is bland to others.

Thus without share in coin or land,
But well content to hold
The wealth of Nature in my hand,
One flail of virgin gold,—
My Love above me like a sun,—
My own bright thoughts my wings,—
Thro' life I trust to flutter on,
As gay as aught that sings.

One hour I own I dread,—to die
Alone and unbefriended,—
No soothing voice, no tearful eye,—
But that must soon be ended ;
And then I shall receive my part
Of everlasting treasure,
In that just world where each man's heart
Will be his only measure.

———

THE VIOLET-GIRL.

WHEN Fancy will continually rehearse
Some painful scene once present to the eye,
'Tis well to mould it into gentle verse,
That it may lighter on the spirit lie.

I

Home yester-eve I wearily returned,
Though bright my morning mood and short my way,
But sad experience in one moment earned,
Can crush the heape'd enjoyments of the day.

Passing the corner of a popu'lous street,
I marked a girl whose wont it was to stand,
With pallid cheek, torn gown, and naked feet,
And bunches of fresh Violets in each hand.

There her small commerce in the chill March weather
She plied with accents miserably mild ;
It was a frightful thought to set together
Those healthy blossoms and that fading child :—

—Those luxuries and largess of the earth,
Beauty and pleasure to the sense of man,
And this poor sorry weed cast loosely forth
On Life's wild waste to struggle as it can !

To me that odo'rous purple ministers
Hope-bearing memories and inspiring glee,
While meanest images alone are hers,
The sordid wants of base humanity.

Think after all this lapse of hungry hours,
In the disfurnished chamber of dim cold,
How she must loathe the very scented flowers
That on the squalid table lie unsold !

Rest on your woodland banks and wither there,
Sweet preluders of Spring ! far better so,
Than live misused to fill the grasp of care,
And serve the piteous purposes of woe.

Ye are no longer Nature's gracious gift,
Yourselves so much and harbingers of more,
But a most bitter irony to lift
The veil that hides our vilest mortal sore.

THE OLD MANORIAL HALL.

WHEN She was born I had been long the garde'ner of the Hall,
The shrubs I planted with my hand were rising thick and tall ;
My heart was in that work and place, and little thought or care
Had I of other living things than grew and flourished there,
   Beneath the happy shelter of
   The old Manorial Hall.

At first she came a rosy child, a queen among my flowers,
And played beside me while I worked, and prattled on for hours ;
And, many a morning, in the plot of ground she called her own,
She found an unexpected show of blossoms freshly blown,
   And sent her merry echoes through
   Her old Manorial Hall.

Thus fifteen summers, every day, I tended her and them,
I watched the opening of the bud, the shooting of the stem ;
And when her childly laughter turned to silent maiden smiles,
I felt in Heaven whene'er she passed, and scarce on earth the whiles.
   How could I ever think to leave
   My old Manorial Hall ?

One day when Autumn's last delights were nipped by early cold,
It fell like Death upon mine ear that She was bought and sold ;—

That some rich lord, she hardly knew, had come to bear away
The pride of all the country round—the poor man's hope and
    stay—
        The glory and the darling of
        Our old Manorial Hall.

I heard her plight to him the troth she could not understand,
I saw her weeping turn her head and wave her parting hand ;
And from that hour no thing on earth has gone with me but
    wrong,
And soon I left the Garden and the Home I loved so long :
        It was a haunted house to me,
        That old Manorial Hall !

And now I wander up and down, I labour as I can,
Without a wish for rest or friends, a sorry-hearted man ;
Yet at the bottom of my thoughts the saddest lies, that She,
With all her wealth and noble state, may none the happier be
        Than I, the poor old Garde'ner of
        The old Manorial Hall.

THE BROOK-SIDE.

    I WANDERED by the brook-side,
    I wandered by the mill,—
    I could not hear the brook flow,
    The noisy wheel was still ;
    There was no burr of grasshopper,
    Nor chirp of any bird,
    But' the beating of my own heart
    Was all the sound I heard.

I sat beneath the elm-tree,
I watched the long, long, shade,
And as it grew still longer,
I did not feel afraid ;
For I listened for a footfall,
I listened for a word,—
But' the beating of my own heart
Was all the sound I heard.

He came not,—no, he came not,—
The night came on alone,—
The little stars sat, one by one,
Each on his golden throne ;
The evening air passed by my cheek,
The leaves above were stirr'd,—
But' the beating of my own heart
Was all the sound I heard.

Fast silent tears were flowing,
When something stood behind,—
A hand was on my shoulder,
I knew its touch was kind :
It drew me nearer—nearer,—
We did not speak one word,
For' the beating of our own hearts
Was all the sound we heard.

LABOUR.

HEART of the People ! Working men !
Marrow and nerve of human powers ;
Who on your sturdy backs sustain
Through streaming Time this world of ours ;
Hold by that title,—which proclaims,
That ye are undismayed and strong,
Accomplishing whatever aims
May to the sons of earth belong.

Yet not on you alone depend
These offices, or burthens fall ;
Labour for some or other end
Is Lord and master of us all.
The high-born youth from downy bed
Must meet the morn with horse and hound,
While Industry for daily bread
Pursues afresh his wonted round.

With all his pomp of pleasure, He
Is but your working comrade now,
And shouts and winds his horn, as ye
Might whistle by the loom or plough ;
In vain for him has wealth the use
Of warm repose and careless joy,—
When, as ye labour to produce,
He strives, as active to destroy.

But who is this with wasted frame,
Sad sign of vigour overwrought ?
What toil can this new victim claim ?
Pleasure, for Pleasure's sake besought.

How men would mock her flaunting shows,
Her golden promise, if they knew
What weary work she is to those
Who have no better work to do !

And He who still and silent sits
In closèd room or shady nook,
And seems to nurse his idle wits
With folded arms or open book :—
To things now working in *that* mind,
Your children's children well may owe
Blessings that Hope has ne'er defined
Till from his busy thoughts they flow.

Thus all must work—with head or hand,
For self or others, good or ill ;
Life is ordained to bear, like land,
Some fruit, be fallow as it will :
Evil has force itself to sow
Where we deny the healthy seed,—
And all our choice is this,—to grow
Pasture and grain or noisome weed.

Then in content possess your hearts,
Unenvious of each other's lot,—
For those which seem the easiest parts
Have travail which ye reckon not :
And He is bravest, happiest, best,
Who, from the task within his span,
Earns for himself his evening rest
And an increase of good for man.

RICH AND POOR.

WHEN God built up the dome of blue,
And portioned earth's prolific floor,
The measure of his wisdom drew
A line between the Rich and Poor;
And till that vault of glory fall,
Or beauteous earth be scarred with flame,
Or saving love be all in all,
That rule of life will rest the same.

We know not why, we know not how,
Mankind are framed for weal or woe—
But to the' Eternal Law we bow;
If such things are, they must be so.
Yet, let no cloudy dreams destroy
One truth outshining bright and clear,
That Wealth abides in Hope and Joy,
And Poverty in Pain and Fear.

Behold our children as they play !
Blest creatures, fresh from Nature's hand ;
The peasant boy as great and gay
As the young heir to gold and land ;
Their various toys of equal worth,
Their little needs of equal care,
And halls of marble, huts of earth,
All homes alike endeared and fair.

They know no better !—would that we
Could keep our knowledge safe from worse ;
So Power should find and leave us free,
So Pride be but the owner's curse ;
So, without marking which was which,
Our hearts would tell, by instinct sure,
What paupers are the' ambitious Rich !
How wealthy the contented Poor !

Grant us, O God ! but health and heart,
And strength to keep desire at bay,
And ours *must* be the better part,
Whatever else besets our way.
Each day may bring sufficient ill ;
But we can meet and fight it through,
If Hope sustains the hand of Will,
And Conscience is our captain too.

CLENT HILL.

ABOVE LORD LYTTELTON'S HOUSE AT HAGLEY.

IF you would mount the hill of Clent,
 And read the fair expanse aright,
Mount ere the autumn moon has spent
 Her lustre on the tepid night :
There on the dewless, close-shorn, grass,
 Remain in vigil'ant repose,
Till objects cease to rise or pass,
 But round your central spirit close.

The moony mist around diffused
  Enlarges all the bounds of space,
And sight, delightfully abused,
  Enjoys the new gigantic grace :
Though here delusion reigns in vain,
  Where the full-bosomed trees combine
With wavy meads that still again
  Meet the far mountain's wavy line.

No sound disturbs the torpid gleam :
  Sleep, happy vales ! sleep, honest souls !
While nature keeps her moonlight dream,
  No darker your good rest controuls ;
Say, rather, meteor stars of hope
  May flash your weary hearts within,
Enabling you at morn to cope
  With day's God-guided discipline.

Yet Night can work as well as Day :
  Behold the' horizon's northern line,
Where huge volcanic masses play
  Red flame against the white moonshine ;
We cannot hear the furnace-roar,
  Nor see the watchful, earnest, hands
That feed the fire and tend the ore,
  Yet feel we what the scene demands.

For it is thus, and thus alone,
  By banded powers of calm and zeal,
By toil and silence blent in one,
  That England shapes her common-weal ;

Thus to the reeking fires of earth
  An elemental work is given,
As pure in purpose, rich in worth,
  As glorifies the orbs of Heaven.

While our poor souls, by Adam's law,
  Would madden with continuous strife,
Nightly from death's abyss we draw
  Regenerate energies of life ;
Oh ! dawn the day, that night has none
  That needs no sleep, and asks no rest,
When we may labour, like the sun,
  In God's great work complete and blest !

———

ON THE

OPENING OF THE FIRST PUBLIC PLEASURE-GROUND AT BIRMINGHAM,

AUGUST, 1856.

I.

SOLDIERS of Industry ! come forth :
  Knights of the Iron Hand !
Past is the menace of the North
  That frowned upon our land.
We have no will to count the cost,
  No thought of what we bore
Now the last warrior's gaze has lost
  The doomed Crimean shore !

II.

That shore, so precious in the graves
　　Of those whose lustrous deeds
Consecrate Balaklava's waves,
　　And Alma's flowe'ring reeds;
Where, at some future festival,
　　Our Russian foe will tell,
How British wrestlers, every fall,
　　Rose stronger than they fell.

III.

Now town and hamlet cheer to see
　　Each bronzed and bearded man,
Or murmur low, " 'Twas such as he,
　　Who died at the Redan!"
Rest for his worn or crippled frame,
　　Rest for his anxious eye,—
Rest, even from the noise of Fame,
　　A Nation's welcome-cry!

IV.

But Ye,—whose resolute intents
　　And sturdy arms combine
To bend the' obdurate elements
　　Of Earth to Man's design—
Ye, to your hot and constant task
　　Heroically true,
Soldiers of Industry! we ask,
　　" Is there no Peace for you?"

V.

It may not be: the' unpausing march
　　Of toil must still be yours—
Conquest, with no triumphant arch,
　　Unsung by Troubadours:

Yet, as the fiercest Knights of old
   To give "God's Truce" agreed,
Cry ye, who are as brave and bold,
   "God's Truce" in Labour's need.

VI.

"God's Truce" be their device, who meet
   To-day with generous zeal
To work, by many a graceful feat,
   Their brethren's future weal;
From stifling street and popu'lous mart
   To guard this ample room,
For honest pleasures kept apart,
   And deck'd with green and bloom.

VII.

Here let the eye to toil minute
   Condemned, with joy behold
The fresh enchantment of each suit
   That clothes the common mould:
Here let the arm whose skilful force
   Controuls such mighty powers,
Direct the infant's totte'ring course
   Amid the fragrant bowers.

VIII.

Yet all in vain this happy hope,
   In vain this friendly care,
Unless of loftier life the scope
   In every mind be there:
In vain the fairest, brightest, scene,
   If passion's sensual haze
And clouded spirits lie between
   To mar the moral gaze.

IX.

He only at the marriage-feast
  Of Nature and of God
Sits worthily who sits released
  From sin's and sorrow's load :
And then, on his poor window-sill,
  One flower more pleasure brings
Than all the gorgeous plants that fill
  The restless halls of kings.

X.

All Nature answers in the tone
  In which she is addressed :
Beneath Mont Blanc's illumined throne,
  The peasant walks unblessed ;
The' Italian struggles in his bonds,
  Beside his glorious sea,
And Beauty from all sight absconds
  Which is not wise and free.

XI.

So, Friends ! while gentle Arts are wed
  To frame your perfect plan,
Broadcast be Truth and Knowledge spread
  O'er this rich soil of Man !
Ideal parks—ideal shade—
  Lay out with libe'ral hand—
But teach the souls you strive to aid
  To feel and understand.

VERSICLES.

AMID the factions of the field of life
The Poet held his little neutral ground,
And they who mixed the deepest in the strife
Their evening way to his seclusion found.

There, meeting oft the' antagonists of the day,
Who near in mute defiance seemed to stand,
He said what neither would be first to say,
And, having spoken, left them hand in hand.

———

I sent my memo'ry out
To chase a Thought :
It brought back doubt on doubt,
But never caught
The fugitive,—who will return some day
When I've no use for him in work or play.

———

The heart that Passion never fired,
Of other's Love can nothing tell—
How can I teach you what's inspired,
Unless you are inspired as well ?

———

Because your nature can extend
Its vision to a needle's end,
And you, with self-sufficient air,
Announce the wonders you see there,—

You must not murmur that some eye
Moulded and trained to range the sky,
May read in yon far star as clear
As you can spy and potter here.

Brothers ! if we return you good
For evil said or malice done,
Doubt not, but in our veins the blood
As hot as in your own may run.

Father ! if bravely we endure
The anguish that with Life begins,
May'st Thou, to whom all things are pure,
Endure our follies and our sins !

Eastward roll the orbs of heaven,
Westward tend the thoughts of men :
Let the Poet, nature-driven,
Wander Eastward now and then :

There the calm of life comparing
With his Europe's busy fate,
Let him, gladly homeward faring,
Learn to labour and to wait.

PALM LEAVES.

THE HAREEM.

BEHIND the veil, where depth is traced
  By many a complicated line,—
Behind the lattice closely laced
  With filagree of choice design,—
Behind the lofty garden-wall,
  Where stranger face can ne'er surprise,—
That inner world her all-in-all,
  The Eastern Woman lives and dies.

Husband and children round her draw
  The narrow circle where she rests ;
His will the single perfect law,
  That scarce with choice her mind molests;
Their birth and tutelage the ground
  And meaning of her life on earth—
She knows not elsewhere could be found
  The measure of a woman's worth.

If young and beautiful, she dwells
  An Idol in a secret shrine,
Where one high-priest alone dispels
  The solitude of charms divine :

K

And in his happiness she lives,
  And in his honour has her own,
And dreams not that the love she gives
  Can be too much for him alone.

Within the gay kiosk reclined,
  Above the scent of lemon groves,
Where bubbling fountains kiss the wind,
  And birds make music to their loves,—
She lives a kind of faëry life,
  In sisterhood of fruits and flowers,
Unconscious of the outer strife,
  That wears the palpitating hours.

And when maturer duties rise
  In pleasure's and in passion's place,
Her duteous loyalty supplies
  The presence of departed grace :
So hopes she, by untiring truth,
  To win the bliss to share with him
Those glories of celestial youth,
  That time can never taint or dim.*

Thus in the ever-closed Hareem,
  As in the open Western home,
Sheds womanhood her starry gleam
  Over our being's busy foam ;
Through latitudes of varying faith
  Thus trace we still her mission sure,
To lighten life, to sweeten death,
  And all for others to endure.

* It is supposed to be left to the will of the husband to decide whether
his wife should be united to him in a future state : but this does not imply
that her happiness after death depends upon him.

Home of the East ! thy threshold's edge
  Checks the wild foot that knows no fear,
Yet shrinks, as if from sacrilege—
  When rapine comes thy precincts near :
Existence, whose precarious thread
  Hangs on the tyrant's mood and nod,
Beneath thy roof its anxious head
  Rests, as within the house of God.

There, though without he feels a slave,
  Compelled another's will to scan,
Another's favour forced to crave—
  There is the Subject still the Man :
There is the form that none but he
  Can touch,—the face that he alone
Of living men has right to see ;—
  Not He who fills the Prophet's throne.

Then let the Moralist, who best
  Honours the female heart, that blends
The deep affections of the West
  With thought of life's sublimest ends,
Ne'er to the Eastern home deny
  Its lesser, yet not humble praise,
To guard one pure humanity
  Amid the stains of evil days.

THE MOSQUE.

A SIMPLE unpartitioned room,—
Surmounted by an ample dome,
Or, in some lands that favoured lie,
With centre open to the sky,
But roofed with archèd cloisters round,
That mark the consecrated bound,
And shade the niche to Mekkeh turned,
By which two massive lights are burned ;
With pulpit, whence the sacred word
Expounded on great days is heard ;
With fountain fresh, where, ere they pray,
Men wash the soil of earth away ;
With shining mina'ret, thin and high,
From whose fine-trelliced balcony
Announcement of the hours of prayer
Is uttered to the silent air ;
Such is the Mosque—the holy place, .
Where faithful men of every race,
Meet at their ease, and face to face.

Not that the power of God is here
More manifest, or more to fear ;
Not that the glory of his face
Is circumscribed by any space ;
But that, as men are wont to meet
In court or chamber, mart or street,

For purposes of gain or pleasure,
For friendliness or social leisure,—
So, for the greatest of all ends
To which intelligence extends,
The worship of the Lord, whose will
Created and sustains us still,
And honour of the Prophet's name,
By whom the saving message came,
Believers meet together here,
And hold these precincts very dear.

The floor is spread with matting neat,
Unstained by touch of shodden feet—
A decent and delightful seat !
Where, after due devotions paid,
And legal ordinance obeyed,
Men may in happy parlance join,
And gay with serious thought combine ;
May ask the news from lands away,
May fix the business of to-day ;
Or, with " God willing," at the close,
To-morrow's hopes and deeds dispose.

Children are running in and out
With silver-sounding laugh and shout,
No more disturbed in their sweet play,
No more disturbing those that pray,
Than the poor birds, that fluttering fly
Among the rafters there on high,
Or seek at times, with grateful hop,
The corn fresh-sprinkled on the top.*

---

* Many of the mosques possess funds dedicated to the support of birds
and other animals : one at Cairo has a large boat at the top filled with

So, lest the stranger's scornful eye
Should hurt this sacred family,—
Lest inconside'rate words should wound
Devout adorers with their sound,—
Lest careless feet should stain the floor
With dirt and dust from out the door,—
'Tis well that custom should protect
The place with prudence circumspect,
And let no unbeliever pass
The threshold of the faithful mass ;
That as each Muslim his Hareem
Guards even from a jealous dream,
So should no alien feeling scathe
This common home of public faith,
So should its very name dispel
The presence of the infidel.

Yet, though such reve'rence may demand
A building raised by human hand,
Most honour to the men of prayer,
Whose mosque is in them everywhere !
Who, amid revel's wildest din,
In war's severest discipline,
On rolling deck, in thronged bazaar,
In stranger lands, however far,
However diffe'rent in their reach
Of thought, in manners, dress, or speech,—
Will quietly their carpet spread,
To Mekkeh turn the humble head,
And, as if blind to all around,
And deaf to each distracting sound,

corn as fast as it is consumed, and another possessed an estate bequeathed
to it to give food to the homeless cats of the city.

In ritual language God adore,
In spirit to his presence soar,
And, in the pauses of the prayer,
Rest, as if rapt in glory there!

THE KIOSK.*

BENEATH the shadow of a large-leaved plane,
Above the ripple of a shallow stream,
Beside a cypress-planted cemetery,
In a gay-painted trellis-worked kiosk,
A company of easy Muslims sat,
Enjoying the calm measure of delight
God grants the faithful even here on earth.
Most pleasantly the bitter berry tastes,
Handed by that bright-eyed and neat-limbed boy;
Most daintily the long chibouk is filled
And almost before emptied, filled again;
Or, with a free good-will, from mouth to mouth
Passes the cool Nargheelee † serpentine.
So sit they, with some low occasional word
Breaking the silence in itself so sweet,
While o'er the neighbou'ring bridge the caravan
Winds slowly in one line interminable
Of camel after camel, each with neck
Jerked up, as sniffing the far desert air.

---

* Story-telling is, now as ever, the delight of the East: in the coffee
and summer houses, at the corners of the streets, in the courts of the
mosque, sit the grave and attentive crowd, hearing with childly pleasure
the same stories over and over again, applauding every new turn of
expression or incident, but not requiring them any more than the hearers
of a European sermon.

† The hookah of the Levant.

Then one serene old Turk, with snow-white beard
Hanging amid his pistol-hilts profuse,
Spoke out—" Till sunset all the time is ours,
And we should take advantage of the chance
That brings us here together.   This my friend
Tells by his shape of dress and peakèd cap
Where his home lies : he comes from furthest off,
So let the round of tales begin with him."
Thus challenged, in his thoughts the Persian dived,
And, with no waste of faint apologies,
Related a plain story of his life,
Nothing adventu'rous, terrible, or strange,
But, as he said, a simple incident,
That any one there present might have known.

THE PERSIAN'S STORY.

" Wakedi, and the Heshemite, and I,
Called each the other friend, and what we meant
By all the meaning of that common word,
One tale among a hundred—one round pearl
Dropped off the chain of daily circumstance
Into the Poet's hand—one luscious fruit
Scarce noticed in the summer of the tree,
Is here preserved, that you may do the like.

" The Ramadhan's long days (where'er they fall
Certain to seem the longest of the year)
Were nearly over, and the populous streets
Were silent as if haunted by the plague ;
For all the town was crowding the bazaar,
To buy new garments, as beseemed the time,
In honour of the Prophet and themselves.

But in our house my wife and I still sat,
And looked with sorrow in each other's faces.
It was not for ourselves—we well could let
Our present clothes serve out another year,
And meet the neighbours' scoffs with quiet minds ;
But for our children we were grieved and shamed ;
That they should have to hide their little heads,
And take no share of pleasure in the Feast,
Or else contrast their torn and squalid vests
With the gay freshness of their playmates' garb.
At last my wife spoke out—' Where are your friends ?
Where is Wakedi ? where the Heshemite ?
That you are worn and pale with want of gold,
And they perchance with coin laid idly by
In some closed casket, or in some vain sport
Wasted, for want of honest purposes ? '
My heart leapt light within me at these words,
And I, rejoicing at my pain as past,
Sent one I trusted to the Heshemite,
Told him my need in few plain written words,
And, ere an hour had passed, received from him
A purse of gold tied up, sealed with his name :
And in a moment I was down the street,
And, in my mind's eye, chose the children's clothes.
—But between will and deed, however near,
There often lies a gulf impassable.
So, ere I reached the gate of the Bazaar,
Wakedi's slave accosted me—his breath
Cut short with haste ; and from his choking throat
His master's message issued word by word.
The sum was this :—a cruel creditor,
Taking the 'vantage of the season's use,
Pressed on Wakedi for a debt, and swore
That, unless paid ere evening-prayer, the law

Should wring by force the last of his demand.
Wakedi had no money in the house,
And I was prayed, in this his sudden strait,
To aid him, in my duty as a friend.
Of course I took the Heshemite's sealed purse
Out of my breast, and gave it to the slave ;
Yet I must own, oppressed with foolish fear
Of my wife's tears, and, might be, bitter words,
If empty-handed I had home returned,
I sat all night, half-sleeping, in the mosque,
Beneath the glimme'ring feathers, eggs, and lamps,
And only in the morning nerved my heart
To tell her of our disappointed pride.
She, when I stammered out my best excuse,
Abashed me with her kind approving calm,
Saying—' The parents' honour clothes the child.'
Thus I grew cheerful in her cheerfulness,
And we began to sort the children's vests,
And found them not so sordid after all.
' This might be turned—that stain might well be hid—
This remnant might be used.'   So we went on
Almost contented, till surprised we saw
The Heshemite approach, and with quick steps
Enter the house, and in his hand he showed
The very purse tied up, sealed with his name,
Which I had given to help Wakedi's need !
At once he asked us, mingling words and smiles,
' What means this secret ? you sent yester morn
Asking for gold, and I, without delay,
Returned the purse containing all I had.
But I too found myself that afternooh
Wanting to buy a sash to grace the feast ;
And sending to Wakedi, from my slave
Received this purse I sent you the same morn

Unopened.' ' Easy riddle,' I replied,
' And, as I hope, no miracle for me—
That what you gave me for my pleasure's fee
Should serve Wakedi in his deep distress.'
And then I told him of Wakedi's fate :
And we were both o'ercome with anxious care
Lest he, obeying his pure friendship's call,
Had perilled his own precious liberty,
Or suffered some hard judgment of the law.
But to our great delight and inward peace,
Wakedi a few moments after stood
Laughing behind us, ready to recount,
How Allah, loving the unshrinking faith
With which he had supplied his friend's desire
Regardless of his own necessity,
Assuaged the creditor's strong rage, and made
His heart accessible to gentle thoughts,
Granting Wakedi time to pay the debt.
—Thus our three tales were gathered into one,
Just as I give them you, and with the purse
Then opened in the presence of the three—
We gave my children unpretending vests,
Applied a portion to Wakedi's debts,
And bought the Heshemite the richest sash
The best silk merchant owned in the Bazaar."

Soon as he ceased, a pleasant murmur rose,
Not only of applause, but of good words,
Dwelling upon the subject of the tale ;
Each to his neighbour in low utte'rance spoke
Of Friendship and its blessings, and God's grace,
By which man is not left alone to fight
His daily battle through a cruel world.

So.
Shou
Lest
Devo
Lest
With
'Tis
The
And
The
That
Guar
So sh
This
So sh
The

Ye
A bu
Most
Who
W
I

My free command of all these tribes of men,
My power to slay or keep alive,—my wealth,
Which once I deemed the envy of all kings,—
If by my life amid these wild waste hills
I am shut out from that deliciousness
Which makes existence heavenly in your words,—
If I must pass into my Father's tomb,
These pleasures all untasted, this bright earth
To me in one dark corner only known?
Why should I not, for some short time, lay by
My heavy sceptre, and with wealth in hand,
And thee to guide and light me in my path,
Travel to those fair countries God-endowed,—
And then with store of happy memories,
And thoughts, for pauses of the lion-hunt,
And tales to tell, to keep the evenings warm,
Return once more to my paternal throne?'
Gladly the merchant, weary with his stay
In that far land, and fearing lest kind force
Might hold him priso'ner there for some long time,
Accepted the proposal, praised the scheme
As full of wise, and just, and manly thought,
Recounted the advantages the land
Would from their King's experience surely draw:
And ended by determining the day
When they two should set out upon their road,
Worthily armed, with ample store of gold,
And gems adroitly hid about their dress.

  " The day arrived, big with such change of life
To this brave Monarch: in barbaric pomp
Were gathered all the princes of the race,
All men of name and prowess in the state,
And tributary chiefs from Ethiop hills.

With mingled admiration and dismay
They heard the King announce he should go forth
To distant nations ere that sun went down ;—
That for two years they would not see his face ;
But then he trusted God he should return
Enriched with wisdom, worthier of his rule,
And able to impart much good to them.
Then to the trust of honorable men
Committing sepa'rate provinces and towns,
And over all, in delegated rule,
Establishing his favou'rite brother's power,
Amid applauses, tumults, prayers, and tears,
Towards the Arabian Gulf he bent his way.
A well-manned boat lay ready on the shore ;
A prospe'rous gale was playing on the sea,
And after some few days of pleasant sail,
From Djedda's port to Mekkeh's blessed walls
The Merchant and the King advanced alone.

" At every step he made in this new world,
At every city where they stopped a while
On their long journey, with the fresh delight
His eye was ravished and his heart was full ;
And when at last upon his vision flashed
Holy Damascus,* with its mosques, and streams,
A gem of green set in the golden sand,
The King embraced his friend ; and, thanking God
That he had led him to this heaven, despised
The large dominion of his Afric birth,
And vowed he'd rather be a plain man there,
Than rule o'er all the sources of the Nile.

---

* Statius (Sylv. 1. 6, 14) speaks of Syrian plums, as, "Quod ramis pia
germinat Damascus."

Thus in Damascus they were safely housed,
And as the King's gold through the Merchant's hands
Flowed freely, friends came pouring in amain,
Deeming it all the fortunate reward
Of the bold Merchant's venture; for he spoke
To none about the secret King, who seemed
Rather some humble fond companion brought
From the far depths of that gold-teeming land.
Oh! what a life of luxury was there!
Velvet divans, curtains of broidered silk,
Carpets, as fine a work of Persian looms
As those that in the Mosque at Mekkeh lie;
The longest, straitest, pipes in all the East,
With amber mouth-pieces as clear as air;
Fresh sparkling sherbet, such as Franks adore;*
And maidens who might dazzle by their charms
The Sultan seated in his full Hareem.
The months rolled on with no diminished joys,
Nay, each more lavish in magnificence
Than that which went before; and, drunk with pleasure,
The Merchant lost all sense and estimate
Of the amount of wealth he and the King
Had brought together from that distant clime.
The gold was soon exhausted, yet remained
A princely store of jewels, which for long
Sustained that fabric of enchanted life,
But one by one were spent and past away;
Then came the covert sale of splendours bought;
Then money borrowed easily at first,
But every time extracted with more pain
From the strong griping clutch of usury.
But all the while, unwitting of the truth,

---

* Our champagne is a favourite sherbet of the East.

Without the faintest shadow of distrust
Of his friend's prudence, care, or honesty,
Taking whatever share of happiness
He gave him with an absolute content,
Tranquil the Abyssinian King remained,
Confiding and delighted as a child.

" At last the hour came on, though long delayed,
When the bare fact before the Merchant's eyes
Stood out, that he was ruined without hope !
What could be done ?   Not only for himself,
But for his friend, that poor deluded King,
Become an useless burthen on his hands ?
He knew his doors, that guests so lately thronged,
Would soon be thronged as thick with creditors ;
And he himself, by law, be forced to pay
In person, where he had no gold to give :
He must escape that very hour—but how ?
Without one good piastre to defray
His cost upon the road, or bribe the porters
To set his creditors on some false scent.
Then rose a thought within him, and, it seemed,
Was gladly welcomed by a sudden start,
And a half-cruel, half-compassionate, smile.
For straight he sought the Abyssinian King,
Whom he found watching with a quiet smile
The gold fish in the fountain gleam and glide.
He led him, ever ductile, by the hand
Down many streets into a close-built court
Where sat together many harsh-browed men,
Whom he accosted thus : ' Friends, I want gold ;
Here is a slave I brought with me last year
From Abyssinia ; he is stout and strong,
And, but for some strange crotchets in his head

Of his own self-importance and fond dreams,
Which want a little waking now and then
By means that you at least know well to use,
A trusty servant and long-headed man ;
Take him at your own price—I have no time
To drive a bargain.' ' Well, so much,'—one cried—
' So much' another. ' Bring your purses out,
You have bid most, and let me count the coin.'
Dumb as a rock the Abyssinian King,
Gathering the meaning of the villany,
Stood for a while ; then, in a frantic burst,
Rushed at his base betrayer, who, his arm
Avoiding, gathered up his gold and fled :
And the slave-merchant, as a man to whom
All wild extremities of agony
Were just as common as his daily bread,
Shouted, and like a felon in a cage
The King was soon forced down by many hands.

" None know what afterwards became of him :
Haply he died, as was the best for him ;
And, but that the false Merchant, proud of crime,
Oft told the story as a good device
And laughable adventure of his craft,
The piteous fate of that deluded King
Had been as little known to any one
As to the subjects of his distant realm,
Who still, perchance, expect their Lord's return,
Laden with all the wealth of Eastern lands."

———

'Twas strange to see how, upon diffe'rent minds
The Syrian's tale with diffe'rent meanings fell.
One moralised of the vicissitudes

L

Of mortal greatness,—how the spider's web
Is just as safe from harm and violence
As the bright-woven destiny of kings.
Another cursed the Merchant for his deed:
And a third laughed aloud and laughed again,
Conside'ring the strange contrast of the pomp
Of that departure from a regal throne
And grand commission of so many powers,
With the condition of a kennelled slave;
For true it is, that nothing moves to mirth
More than the gap that fortune often leaps,
Dragging some wretched man along with her.

To an Egyptian soldier, scarred and bronzed,
The duty of narration came the next:
Who said, "that soldiers' tales were out of place
Told in calm places and at evening hours:
His songs required the music of the gun:
He could recount a thousand despe'rate feats,
Hair-breadth escapes and miracles of war,
Were he but cowe'ring round a low watch-fire
Almost in hearing of the enemy;
But now his blood was cold, and he was dull,
And even had forgot his own wild past.
They all had heard—had East and West not heard
Of Mehemet Ali and of Ibrahim?
It might be that the Great Pasha was great,
But he was fond of trade—of getting gold,
Not by fair onslaught and courageous strength,
But by mean interchange with other lands
Of produce better in his own consumed;
This was like treason to a soldier's heart;
And all he hoped was that when Ibrahim
Sat in his father's seat, he would destroy

That flight of locusts—Jew, and Greek, and Frank,
Who had corrupted Egypt and her power,
By all their mercenary thoughts and acts,
And sent him there, brave soldier as he was,
To go beg service at the Sultan's hand.
Yet Ibrahim's heart was still a noble one ;
No man could contradict him and not fear
Some awful vengeance ;—was this story known ?"

————

THE EGYPTIAN'S STORY.

Once, when in Syria he had let war loose,
And was reducing, under one strong sway,
Druses, and Christians, and Mohammedans,
He heard that his last child, the favourite
Born of a favou'rite wife, had been let fall
By a young careless Nubian nurse, and hurt,
So as to cripple it through all its days.
No word of anger passed the warrior's lips,—
No one would think the story on his mind
Rested a single moment.   But due time
Brought round his glad return, and he once more
Entered his hall, within which, on each side,
Long marble stairs curved towards the balcony,
Where right and left the women's chambers spread ;
Upon the landing stood the glad Hareem
To welcome him with music, shouts, and songs ;
Yet he would not ascend a single step,
But cried—" Where is the careless Nubian girl
That let my child fall on the stony ground?"
Trembling and shrieking down one marble flight
She was pushed forward, till she reached the floor :

L 2

Then Ibrahim caught her in one giant grasp,
Dragged her towards him, and one brawny hand
Tight-twisting in her long and glossy hair,
And with the other drawing the sharp sword
Well known at Nezib and at Koniah,
Sheer from her shoulders severed the young head,
And casting it behind him, at few bounds
Cleared the high stair and to his bosom pressed
The darling wife his deed had just reveng'd.
O! he is god-like in his hour of rage!
His wrath is like the plague that falls on man
With indiscriminate fury, and for this
His name is honoured through the spacious East,
Where all things powerful meet their just reward."

The Soldier paused; and surely some one else
Had taken up the burden of a tale;
But at that moment through the cypress stems
Shot the declining crimson of the sun
Full on the faces of that company,
Who for some instants in deep silence watched
The last appearance of the ruddy rim,
And, little needing the clear warning voice
Which issued round the neighbou'ring minaret,—
Bidding all earthly thoughts and interests
Sink in their breasts as sunk that fiery sun—
Bowed, old and young, their heads in blest accord,
Believers in one Prophet and one God!

THE TENT.

WHY should a man raise stone and wood
  Between him and the sky?
Why should he fear the brotherhood
  Of all things from on high?
Why should a man not raise his form
  As shelterless and free
As stands in sunshine or in storm
  The mountain and the tree?

Or if we thus, as creatures frail,
  Before our time should die,
And courage and endurance fail
  Weak Nature to supply;—
Let us at least a dwelling choose,
  The simplest that can keep
From parching heat and noxious dews
  Our pleasure and our sleep.

The Fathers of our mortal race,
  While still remembrance nursed
Traditions of the glorious place
  Whence Adam fled accursed,—
Rested in tents, as best became
  Children, whose mother earth
Had overspread with sinful shame
  The beauty of her birth.

In cold they sought the sheltered nook,
  In heat the airy shade,
And oft their casual home forsook
  The morrow it was made ;
Diverging many separate roads,
  They wandered, fancy-driven,
Nor thought of other fixed abodes
  Than Paradise or Heaven.

And while this holy sense remained,
  'Mid easy shepherd cares,
In tents they often entertained
  The Angels unawares:
And to their spi'rits fervid gaze
  The myste'ry was revealed,
How the world's wound in future days
  Should by God's love be healed.

Thus we, so late and far a link
  Of generation's chain,
Delight to dwell in tents and think
  The old world young again ;
With Faith as wide and Thought as narrow
  As theirs, who little more
From life demanded than the sparrow
  Gay-chirping by the door.

The Tent ! how easily it stands,
  Almost as if it rose
Spontaneous from the green or sand,
  Express for our repose :

Or, rather, it is we who plant
  This root, where'er we roam,
And hold, and can to others grant,
  The comforts of a home.

Make the Divan—the carpets spread,
  The ready cushions pile ;
Rest, weary heart ! rest, weary head !
  From pain and pride awhile :
And all your happiest memories woo,
  And mingle with your dreams
The yellow desert glimme'ring through
  The subtle veil of beams.

We all have much we would forget—
  Be that forgotten now !
And placid Hope, instead, shall set
  Her seal upon your brow :
Imagination's prophet eye
  By her shall view unfurled
The future greatnesses that lie
  Hid in the Eastern world.

To slavish tyrannies their term
  Of terror she foretells ;
She brings to bloom the faith whose germ
  In Islam deeply dwells ;
Accomplishing each mighty birth
  That shall one day be born
From marriage of the western earth
  With nations of the morn !

Then fold the Tent—then on again ;
   One spot of ashen black,
The only sign that here has lain
   The traveller's recent track :
And gladly forward, safe to find
   At noon and eve a home,
Till we have left our Tent behind,
   The homeless ocean-foam !

———

THE THINKER AND THE POET.

SUNSHINE often falls refulgent
After all the corn is in ;
Often Allah grants indulgent
Pleasure that may guard from sin :
Hence your wives may number four ;
Though he best consults his reason,
Best secures his house from treason,
Who takes one and wants no more.

Nor less well the man once gifted
With one high and holy Thought,
Will not let his mind be shifted,
But adores it, as he ought ;
Well for him whose spirit's youth
Rests as a contented lover,
Nor can other charms discover
Than in his absorbing Truth !

But the heaven-enfranchised Poet
Must have no exclusive home,
He must feel, and freely show it,—
Phantasy is made to roam :
He must give his passions range,
He must serve no single duty,
But from Beauty pass to Beauty,
Constant to a constant change.

With all races, of all ages,
He must people his Hareem ;
He must search the tents of sages,
He must scour the vales of dream :
Ever adding to his store,
From new cities, from new nations,
He must rise to new creations,
And, unsated, ask for more.

In the manifold, the various,
He delights, as Nature's child,—
Grasps at joys the most precarious,
Rides on hopes, however wild !
Though his heart at times perceives
One enduring Love hereafter,
Glimmering through his tears and laughter,
Like the sun through autumn leaves.

LOSS AND GAIN.

MYRIAD Roses, unregretted, perish in their vernal bloom,
That the essence of their sweetness *once* your Beauty may per-
fume.

Myriad Veins of richest life-blood empty forth their priceless
worth,
To exalt *one* Will imperial over spacious realms of earth.

Myriad Hearts are pained and broken that *one* Poet may be
taught
To discern the shapes of passion and describe them as he ought.

Myriad Minds of heavenly temper pass as passes moon or star,
That *one* philosophic Spirit may ascend the solar car.

Sacrifice and Self-devotion hallow earth and fill the skies,
And the meanest Life is sacred whence the highest may arise.

PLEASURE AND PAIN.

WHO can determine the frontier of Pleasure?
Who can distinguish the limit of Pain?
Where is the moment the feeling to measure?
When is experience repeated again?

Ye who have felt the delirium of passion—
    Say, can ye sever its joys and its pangs?
Is there a power in calm contemplation
    To indicate each upon each as it hangs?

I would believe not ;—for spirit may languish
    While sense is most blest and creation most bright ;
And life may be dearer and clearer in anguish
    Than ever was felt in the throbs of delight.

See the Fakèer as he swings on his iron,
    See the thin Hermit that starves in the wild ;
Think ye no pleasures the penance environ,
    And hope the sole bliss by which pain is beguiled?

No ! in the kingdoms those spirits are reaching,
    Vain are our words the emotions to tell ;
Vain the distinctions our senses are teaching,
    For Pain has its Heaven and Pleasure its Hell !

THE PEACE OF GOD.

'The blessed shall hear no vain words, but only the word—Peace.
                    KURAN, chap. xix. v. 63.

PEACE is God's direct assurance
    To the souls that win release
From this world of hard endurance—
    Peace—he tells us—only Peace.

There is Peace in lifeless matter—
　There is Peace in dreamless sleep—
Will then Death our being shatter
　In annihilation's deep?

Ask you this? O mortal trembler!
　Hear the Peace that Death affords,
For your God is no dissembler,
　Cheating you with double words:

To this life's inquiring traveller,
　Peace of knowledge of all good,—
To the anxious truth-unraveller,
　Peace of wisdom understood,—

To the loyal wife, affection
　Towards her husband, free from fear,—
To the faithful friend, selection
　Of all memo'ries kind and dear,—

To the lover, full fruition
　Of an unexhausted joy,—
To the warrior, crowned ambition,
　With no envy's base alloy,—

To the ruler, sense of action,
　Working out his great intent,—
To the prophet, satisfaction
　In the mission he was sent,—

To the poet, conscious glory
　Flowing from his Father's face;—
Such is Peace in holy story,
　Such is Peace in heavenly grace.

RABIA. *

ROUND holy Rabia's suffering bed
  The wise men gathered, gazing gravely—
" Daughter of God ! " the youngest said,
  Endure thy Father's chastening bravely ;
They who have steeped their souls in prayer
Can every anguish calmly bear."

She answered not, and turned aside,
  Though not reproachfully nor sadly ;
" Daughter of God ! " the eldest cried,
  " Sustain thy Father's chastening gladly,
They who have learnt to pray aright,
From pain's dark well draw up delight."

Then she spoke out,—" Your words are fair ;
  But, oh ! the truth lies deeper still ;
I know not, when absorbed in prayer,
  Pleasure or pain, or good or ill ;
They who God's face can understand
Feel not the motions of His hand."

* Rabia was a holy woman, who lived in the second century of the
Hegira. Her sayings and thoughts are collected by many devotional
Arabic writers: they are a remarkable development of a Christian
mystical spirit early in the history of Islam.

THE GREEK AT CONSTANTINOPLE.

THE cypresses of Scutari
  In stern magnificence look down
On the bright lake and stream of sea,
  And glitte'ring theatre of town :
Above the throng of rich kiosks,
  Above the towers in triple tire,
Above the domes of loftiest mosques,
  These pinnacles of death aspire.

It is a wilderness of tombs,—
  Where white and gold and brilliant hue
Contrast with Nature's gravest glooms,
  As these again with heaven's clear blue :
The city's multitudinous hum,
  So far, yet strikes the listening ear,—
But what are thousands to the sum
  Of millions calmly sleeping here ?

For here, whate'er his life's degree,
  The Muslim loves to rest at last,
Loves to recross the band of sea
  That parts him from his people's past.
'Tis well to live and lord o'er those
  By whom his sires were most renowned,
But his fierce heart finds best repose
  In this traditionary ground.

From this funereal forest's edge
  I gave my sight full range below,
Reclining on a grassy ledge,
  Itself a grave, or seeming so :
And that huge city flaunting bright,
  That crowded port and busy shore,
With roofs and minarets steeped in light,
  Seemed but a gaudy tomb the more.

I thought of what one might have hoped
  From Greek and Roman power combined,
From strength, that with a world had coped,
  Matched to the queen of human mind ;—
From all the wisdom, might, and grace,
  That Fancy's gods to man had given,
Blent in one empire and one race,
  By the true faith in Christ and Heaven.

The finest webs of earthly fate
  Are soonest and most harshly torn ;
The wise could scarce discriminate
  That evening splendour from the morn ;
Though we, sad students of the past,
  Can trace the lurid twilight line
That lies between the first and last,
  Who bore the name of Constantine.

Such were my thoughts and such the scene,
  When I perceived that by me stood
A Grecian youth of earnest mien,
  Well-suiting my reflective mood :

And when he spoke, his words were tuned
  Harmonious to my present mind,
As if his spirit had communed
  With mine, while I had there reclined.

"Stranger! whose soul hath strength to soar
  Beyond the compass of the eye,
And on a spot like this can more
  Than charms of form and hue descry,—
Take off this mask of beauty,—scan
  The face of things with truth severe,
Think, as becomes a Christian man,
  Of us thy Christian brethren here!

"Think of that age's awful birth,
  When Europe echoed, terror-riven,
That a new foot was on the earth,
  And a new name come down from Heaven:
When over Calpe's straits and steeps
  The Moor had bridged his royal road,
And Othman's sons from Asia's deeps
  The conquests of the Cross o'erflowed.

"Think, if the arm of Charles Martel
  Had failed upon the plain of Tours,
The fate, whose course you know so well,
  This foul subjection had been yours:
Where then had been the long renown
  France can from sire to son deliver?
Where English freedom rolling down,
  One widening, one continuous, river?

" Think with what passionate delight
  The tale was told in Christian halls,
How Sobieski turned to flight
  The Muslim from Vienna's walls :
How, when his horse triumphant trod
  The burgher's richest robes upon,
The ancient words rose loud—' From God
  A man was sent whose name was John.' *

" Think not that time can ever give
  Prescription to such doom as ours,
That Grecian hearts can ever live
  Contented serfs of barbarous powers :
More than six hundred years had past,
  Since Moorish hosts could Spain o'erwhelm,
Yet Boabdil was thrust at last,
  Lamenting, from Grenada's realm.

" And if to his old Asian seat,
  From this usurped unnatu'ral throne,
The Turk is driven, 'tis surely meet
  That we again should hold our own :
Be but Byzantium's native sign
  Of Cross on Crescent† once unfurled,
And Greece shall guard by right divine
  The portals of the Eastern world.

* Historical.

† The Turks adopted the sign of the Crescent from Byzantium after
the conquest: the Cross above the Crescent is found on many ruins of the
Grecian city; among others, on the Genoese castle on the Bosphorus.
The Virgin standing on the Crescent is another common sign.

M

" Before the small Athenian band
  The Persian myriads stood at bay,
The spacious East lay down unmanned
  Beneath the Macedonian's sway :
Alas ! that Greek could turn on Greek—
  Fountain of all our woes and shame—
Till men knew scarcely where to seek
  The fragments of the Grecian name.

" Know ye the Romans of the North ?
  The fearful race whose infant strength
Stretches its arms of conquest forth,
  To grasp the world in breadth and length ?
They cry ' That ye and we are old,
  And worn with luxuries and cares,
And they alone are fresh and bold,
  Time's latest and most honoured heirs !

" Alas for you ! alas for us !
  Alas for men that think and feel,
If once beside this Bosphorus
  Shall stamp Sclavonia's frozen heel !
Oh ! place us boldly in the van,
  And ere we yield this narrow sea,
· The past shall hold within its span
  At least one more Thermopylæ."

OCCASIONAL POEMS.

A MONUMENT FOR SCUTARI.

"THE cypresses of Scutari
  In stern magnificence look down
On the bright lake and stream of sea
  And glittering theatre of town;
Above the throng of rich kiosks,
  Above the towers in triple tire,
Above the domes of loftiest mosques,
  Those pinnacles of death aspire."

Thus, years ago, in grave descant,
  The trave'ller sang those ancient trees
That Eastern grace delights to plant
  In reverence of man's obsequies;
But time has shed a golden haze
  Of memory round the cypress glooms,
And gladly he reviews the days
  He wandered 'mid those alien tombs.

Now other passion rules the soul;
  And Scutari's familiar name
Arouses thoughts beyond controal,
  A tangled web of pride and shame;

No more shall that fair word recall
  The Moslem and his Asian rest,
But the dear brothers of us all
  Rent from their mother's bleeding breast.

Calmly our warriors moulder there,
  Uncoffined, in the sandy soil,
Once festered in the sultry glare,
  Or wasted in the wintry toil.
No verdure on those graves is seen,
  No shade obstructs the garish day;
The tender dews to keep them green
  Are wept, alas! too far away;

Are wept in homes their smiles shall bless
  No more, beyond the welte'ring deep,
In cottages now fatherless
  On English mead or Highland steep,
In palaces by common grief
  Made level with the meanest room,—
One agony, and one relief—
  The conscience of a glorious doom!

For *there*, too, is Thermopylæ ;—
  As on the dank Ægean shore,
By this bright portal of the sea
  Stood the Devoted as of yore;
When Greece herself was merged in night,
  The Spartan held his honour's meed—
And shall no pharos shed the light
  To future time of Britain's deed?

Masters of Form !—if such be now—
  On sense and powers of Art intent,
To match this mount of sorrow's brow
  Devise your seemliest monument :
One that will symbolize the cause
  For which this might of manhood fell,
Obedience to their country's laws,
  And duty to God's truth as well.

Let, too, the old Miltonic Muse,
  That trumpeted " the scattered bones
Of saints on Alpine mountains," use
  Reveillé of forgotten tones ;
Let some one, worthy to be priest
  Of this high altar of renown,
Write in the tongues of West and East
  Who bore this cross, who wore this crown.

Write that, as Britain's peaceful sons
  Luxurious rich, well-tended poor,
Fronted the foeman's steel and guns,
  As each would guard his household door ;
So, in those ghastly halls of pain
  Where thousand hero-sufferers lay,
Some smiled in thought to fight again,
  And most unmurmu'ring passed away.

Write that, when pride of human skill
  Fell prostrate with the weight of care,
And men prayed out for some strong will,
  Some reason 'mid the wild despair,

The loving heart of woman rose
  To guide the hand and clear the eye,
Gave hope amid the sternest woes,
  And saved what man had left to die.

Write every name—lowlier the birth,
  Loftier the death!—and trust that when
On this regenerated earth
  Rise races of ennobled men,
They will remember—these were they
  Who strove to make the nations free,
Not only from the sword's brute sway,
  But from the spirit's slavery.

––––––

ON THE PEACE,

MAY, 1856.

COME in wild Hopes! that towards the dawning East
Uprose so high; now be content to stand,
Like hooded hawks upon the falconer's hand,
Awhile expectant of the promised feast.
Peace is proclaimed! the captives are releast!
Yet yearns the exile from the alien strand,—
Yet chafes and struggles Europe's fairest land,—
Untamed by priestly kings or kingly priest.
O blessed Peace! if peace were peace indeed,—
Based upon justice and the eternal laws
Which make the free intent of Man the cause
Of all enduring thought and virtuous deed.
But 'tis not so: we know we do but pause,
Awaiting fiercer strife and nobler meed.

CHINA, 1857.

THE little Athens from its pillared hill
Yet reigns o'er spacious tracts of human mind:
Britain, within her narrow bounds confined,
Bends East and West to her sagacious will:
While, recordless alike for good or ill,
China extends her name o'er so much rind
Of the round earth, and only stunts mankind
To mean desires, low acts, and puny skill.
Enormous masses of monotonous life!
Teaching how weak is mere material power
To roll our world toward its heavenly goal:
Teaching how vain is each exhausted hour
That does not mingle in the mental strife,
That does not raise or purify the soul.

IRELAND, 1847.

THE woes of Ireland are too deep for verse:
The Muse has many sorrows of her own;
Griefs she may well to sympathy rehearse,
Pains she may soften by her gentle tone.

But the stark death in hunger and sharp cold,
The slow exhaustion of our mortal clay,
Are not for her to touch.—She can but fold
Her mantle o'er her head, and weep and pray.

O gracious Ruler of the rolling hours!
Let not this agony last over long;
Restore a nation to its manly powers,
Give back its suffe'rings to the sphere of Song.

ENGLAND'S SUMMER, 1857.

THE echoes of the rage of war
  Fade in the Eastern distance;
"Two years ago" looms very far
  In our well-filled existence:
On that broad East, yet more remote,
  We waste not thought or feeling,
But muse on British flags afloat,
  And swarthy millions kneeling.

Week after week the summer sun,
  Undimmed by cloud or shower,
With an Italian speed brings on
  The happy harvest hour;
The arts of peace, by plenty nurst,
  Proclaim the world's alliance,
Even in the merry trumpet-burst,
  And shouts of gay defiance.

Then flash along the sentient-wire
  Some words so brief and fearful,
That they who hear them scarce desire
  To see their children cheerful:
Tidings that through wide Hindostan,
  Where Britain's rule stood surest
No life is safe of Christian man,
  The loftiest or the poorest.

Is it a nation roused to meet
  In arms a strange dominion ?—
A people maddened by the heat
  Of just or false opinion ?
No ; soldiers, cared for as our sons,
  And clothed with England's honour,
Have turned their parricidal guns
  With basest craft upon her !

Soon things that make young blood run cold
  We whisper, while we tremble ;
Or cry " that truths shall not be told
  We to ourselves dissemble ; "
And hideous images affright
  Our soul's deep hiding-places,
And in our sleep we start at sight
  Of unknown forms and faces.

Our fair expanse of green and gold
  Can hardly find us grateful,
The very sun that could behold
  Such scenes is almost hateful ;
Warm rays flare up to cruel heat,—
  We sicken and we languish,
With those on whose sad heads they beat
  Intolerable anguish !

We mark, as comes the breeze of morn
  To freshen and to sweeten
The ripples of the oaten corn,
  The billows of the wheaten,—

And feel that not one such sweet breath
  Can reach where parch'd and tangled
The earth gives up to wasting death
  Our brethren foully mangled.

And oh ! the pangs of those who know
  What never must be spoken—
Hearts that will bear about the woe
  Of memo'ry until broken :
God give them thoughts of those who died
  In Christendom's first ages,—
The child, the veteran, and the bride,—
  The saints of history's pages !

For these are Christian martyrs too
  And England's all the dearer :
The mighty work she has to do
  These agonies brings nearer ;—
Conjuring her by that pure blood
  No moment to abandon
The task of world-embracing good
  She once has laid her hand on.

She cannot match the devilish deed,
  Nor mate the hideous treason,—
Her blow is not the traitor's meed,
  But self-defending reason :
That will be lavish of its life,
  And hold all cost uncounted
Till through the length and breadth of strife
  This peril be surmounted.

Then may she pardon—only then—
  When, shamed and conscience-stricken,
The credulous or slothful men
  Who let the horror thicken—
Who little knew and nothing planned
  The evil bond to sever,
Nor dared to burst it with the hand
  Of resolute endeavour.

Yet while the rulers we condemn,
  Who failed in due prevision,
We trust for Britain, as for them,
  In history's great decision,—
That subject lands more justly ruled,
  And strength more mildly wielded,
Had never been, than when befooled
  To noble hopes we yielded ;—

Hopes of a world the force of law,
  The worth of knowledge prizing ;—
From Heathendom's debasing awe
  To Christian reverence rising ;
Hopes of a people struggling forth
  From custom's deep entrancement,
Led by the conquerors of the North
  To Freedom's safe advancement.

Be this an Oriental tale
  By Saxon pride engendered,—
Hopes for a hundred years may fail,
  Yet not be all surrendered :

And now from each distracting scene
　　Of passion fiercely nourished,
We know what India might have been
　　Had Moslem tyrants flourished:

So would have been, and yet would be,
　　If England shrank from duty.
. . Then watch your harvest wealth with glee ;
　　Rejoice in Nature's beauty,
Making her bounties ministers
　　Of toil and self-denial,
And Victo'ry's surest harbingers,
　　After the fiery trial.

————

COLUMBUS AND THE MAY-FLOWER.*

O LITTLE fleet ! that on thy quest divine
Sailedst from Palos one bright autumn morn,
Say, has old Ocean's bosom ever borne
A freight of Faith and Hope to match with thine ?

Say, too, has Heaven's high favour given again
Such consummation of desire, as shone
About Columbus, when he rested on
The new-found world and married it to Spain ?

Answer—Thou refuge of the Freeman's need,—
Thou for whose destinies no kings looked out,
Nor sages to resolve some mighty doubt,—
Thou simple May-Flower of the salt-sea mead !

* Written as prefatory stanzas to Hunter's collection concerning the Founders of New Plymouth.

When Thou wert wafted to that distant shore—
Gay flowers, bright birds, rich odours, met thee not :
Stern Nature hail'd thee to a sterner lot.—
God gave free earth and air, and gave no more.

Thus to men cast in that heroic mould
Came Empire such as Spaniard never knew—
Such Empire as beseems the just and true ;
And at the last, almost unsought, came Gold.

But He who rules both calm and stormy days
Can guard that people's heart, that nation's health,
Safe on the perilo'us heights of power and wealth,
As in the straitness of the ancient ways.

AN ENVOY TO AN AMERICAN LADY.

BEYOND the vague Atlantic deep,
Far as the farthest prairies sweep,
Where forest-glooms the nerve appal,
Where burns the radiant Western fall,
One duty lies on old and young,—
With filial piety to guard,
As on its greenest native sward,
The glory of the English tongue.
That ample speech !   That subtle speech !
Apt for the need of all and each :
Strong to endure, yet prompt to bend
Wherever human feelings tend.
Preserve its force—expand its powers ;
And through the maze of civic life,
In Letters, Commerce, even in Strife,
Forget not it is yours and ours.

ENGLAND AND AMERICA, 1863.

WE only know that in the sultry weather,
Men toiled for us as in the steaming room,
And in our minds we hardly set together
The bondman's penance and the freeman's loom.

We never thought the jealous gods would store
For us ill deeds of time-forgotten graves,
Nor heeded that the May-Flower one day bore
A freight of pilgrims, and another slaves.

First on the bold upholders of the wrong,
And last on us, the heavy-laden years
Avenge the cruel triumphs of the strong—
Trampled affections, and derided tears.

Labour, degraded from her high behest,
Cries " Ye shall know I am the living breath,
And not the curse of Man.   Ye shall have Rest—
The rest of Famine and the rest of Death."

Oh, happy distant hours ! that shall restore
Honour to work, and pleasure to repose,
Hasten your steps, just heard above the war
Of wildering passions and the crash of foes.

THE FUNERAL OF NAPOLEON.

ALL nature is stiff in the chill of the air,.
The sun looks around with a smile of despair ;
'Tis a day of delusion, of glitter and gloom,
As brilliant as glory, as cold as the tomb.

The pageant is passing—the multitude sways—
Awaiting, pursuing, the line with its gaze,
With the tramp of battalion,. the tremor of drums,
And the grave exultation of trumpets he comes.

It passes ! what passes ?. He comes ! who is He ?
Is it Joy too profound to be uttered in glee ?
Oh, no ! it is Death, the Dethroner of old,
Now folded in purple and girded with gold !

It is Death, who enjoys the magnificent car,
It is Death, whom the warriors have brought from afar,
It is Death, to whom thousands have knelt on the shore,
And sainted the bark and the treasure it bore.

What other than He, in his terrible calm,
Could mingle for myriads the bitter and balm,
Could hush into silence this ocean of men,
And bid the wild passion be. still in its den ?

What other than He could have placed side by side
The chief and the humblest, that serving him died,
Could the blood of the past to the mourner atone,
And let all bless the name that has orphaned their own ?

From the shades of the olive, the palm, and the pine,
From the banks of the Moskwa, the Nile, and the Rhine,
From the sands and the glaciers, in armament dim,
Come they who have perished for France and for Him.

Rejoice, ye sad Mothers, whose desolate years
Have been traced in the desert of earth by their tears,
The Children for whom ye have hearts that still burn,
In this triumph of Death—it is they that return.

And Ye in whose breast dwell the images true
Of parents that loved Him still better than you,
No longer lament o'er a cenotaph urn,
In this triumph of Death—it is they that return.

From legion to legion the watchword is sped—
"Long life to the Emperor—life to the dead!"
The prayer is accomplished—his ashes remain
'Mid the people he loved, on the banks of the Seine.

In dominions of Thought that no traitor can reach,
Through the kingdoms of Fancy, the regions of Speech,
O'er the world of Emotions, Napoleon shall reign
'Mid the people he loved, on the banks of the Seine.

PARIS, December, 1840.

MEMORIALS OF TRAVEL.

THE ELD.

> " To me .   .   .
> Pushed from his chair of regal heritage,
> The Present is the vassal of the Past."
> TENNYSON.

Oh, blessèd, blessèd be the Eld,
  Its echoes and its shades,—
The tones that from all time outswelled,
  The light that never fades ;—
The silver-pinion'd memories,
  The symbol and the tale,—
The soul-enchasèd melodies
  Of merriment or bale.

Oh, glory ! that we wrestle
  So valiantly with Time,
And do not alway nestle
  In listlessness or crime :
We do not live and die
  Irrevocably blind,
But raise our hands and sigh
  For' the might we left behind.

Each goodly sign and mystic letter,
  That angel-haunted books unfold,—
We cherish more,—we know them better,
  When we remember they are old ;

And friends, though fresh, and hale, and cheerly,
  And young, as annals hold,
Yet, if we prize them *very* dearly,
  We love to call them old.

Yon scented shrub,—I passed it by,
  The youngling of the breeze ;
I sat me, sad and soberly,
  Beneath those ancient trees,
Whose branches, dight in summer pall,
  Their gloom in moaning wore ;
For' they told me of the Eld and all
  The mystery of yore.

And in the gusts, I thought they pitied
  The falling of the young,—
The fair, the subtle-witted,
  Fine limb, and honeyed tongue ;—
As man, from birth to funeral,
  Were but a tragic mime,—
And, they the kinsman lineal
  Of' the good and olden prime.

I saw the hoary bulk of ocean
  A' couching on the shore,
With' a ripple for its motion,
  And' a murmur for its roar ;
I gazed, but not as on the dead,
  But as if Death were held
In awe, by a thing that slumberèd
  In the deep and silent Eld.

The golden school of Eld is rife
   With many a God-sent ray,
And jewel-gleams of perfect life,
   Hereditary day!
Alas! we cannot quite awake,—
   But when we feel we dream,
That hour, our heart is strong to shake
   The falsities that seem.

For' our bark is on the angle
   Of' a wide and bending stream,
Whose bosky banks entangle
   The eye's divergent beam ;—
The ridgy steeps hide in the way,
   Whither the stream is quest,
As on a lake, the mirror'd day
   Repeats its waveless rest.

How know we, when so clearly still,
   Where' its nether fountains be?
That' it welleth in a viewless hill,
   And passeth to the sea?
The tide beneath us !—where it welled
   Dull sense regardeth not,—
But it was once the tide of Eld,
   And we' have not all forgot.

Great Art hath bound a diadem,
   Upon his front serene,
Whose every pure and charmèd gem
   Bedews him with its sheen ;

And thus,—nor deem it wildly new,
　Nor slur of idle tongue,—
But true, as God's own words are true,
　The Eld is alway young ;—

Young as the flush of all-blue light,
　Or eve's imperial eyes,—
And he who worshippeth aright,
　Shall aye be young and wise,
And gentle as the virgin dove
　That primal chaos quelled,
With Nature for his ladie-love,
　The daughter of the Eld.

September, 1832.

GREEK RELIGION.

Could we, but for one hour, burst through those gates ada-
　matine,
Which, as the children of men pass onward in swift generation,
Time's dark cavern along, are heavily closing behind them !
Could we but breathe the delight of the time when, fresh in his
　boyhood,
Out of his own exuberant life, Man gave unto Nature,
Till new senses awoke, through every nerve of creation !
Waves of the old Ægean !—I listen your musical ebbing ;
Smile to my eye, as you will, with smiles clear-crystal as ever,
Bind, in your silvery net, fair capes and embowerèd islands ;
But ye can bear no more on your breast that vision of glory,
When in the cool moon-dew went forth the imperial revel,

Dolphins and pearl-shell cars, of the Queen and the People of
    Ocean ;
Whose sweet-undulant murmur the homeless mariner hearkened,
Over the undulant sapphire, and trembled in glad adoration.

How were ye voiced, ye Stars !—how cheerily Castor and Pollux
Spoke to the quivering seaman, amid the outpouring of tempest !
With what a firm-set gaze on the belt triple-gemmed of Orion
Looked the serene Greek child, as he thought of the suffering
    giant,
Panting with sightless orbs for the dawn's miraculous healing !
With what a sigh did he pass from the six proud deified sisters,
On to the fate of the fallen, and mourned for the love that
    dethroned her !
Not by elaborate charts did he read that book of the Heavens,
But to his heart's fine ear it was taught by a heavenly master.

Now from her window perchance may the maiden of desolate
    Hellas,
When with the woes of her love and her land her spirit is
    heavy,
Yearn to the white-bright moon, which, over the curvèd horizon,
Climbing the air still flushed with the flames of the opposite
    sunset,
Seems with affectionate eye to regard her, and weep to her
    weeping ;
Yet is it now not as when, having pined for Endymion's kindness,
She with the mourners of love held personal sympathy ever,
When, in the sky's void chasms a wanderer, she to the pilgrim
Over the world's sick plain was a dear companion in sorrow.

Down through the blue-grey thyme, which roofs their courses
    with odour,
Rivulets, gentle as words from the lips of Beauty, are flowing ;

Still, in the dusky ravine, they deepen and freshen their
waters,
Still, in the thick-arched coves, they slumber and dimple de-
lighted,
Catching the full-swelled fig and the deep-stained arbutus
ruby,—
Still, to the sea's sand-brim, by royally gay oleanders,
And oriental array of reeds, they are ever attended ;
But they are all dumb forms, unimpregnate with vital emotion,
While, from the pure fount-head, no Nymph, her bosom ex-
panding,
Dazzles the way-worn wretch with the smile of her bland bene-
diction,
Giving the welcomed draught mysterious virtue and savour ;—
While no curious hind in the noon-tide's magical ardour,*
Peeps through the blossomy trellice, that over the pool's dark
crystal
Guards the immaculate forms of the awful Olympian bathers ;
While at the wide stream-mouth never one, one, amorous Triton
Breathes to the surge and the tall marsh-blooms euphonious
passion.

These high Temples around, the religious shade of the olive
Falls on the grass close-wove ;—in the redolent valley beneath us,
Stems of the loftiest platain their crowns large-leavèd are spread-
ing,
While the most motley of herds is adorning the calm of their
umbrage ;—
Yet ye are gone, ye are vanished for ever, ye guardian Beings !
Who, in the time-gnarled trunks, broad branches, and summer
enchantment

---

* On the mystical power of noon in the appearance of supernatural beings,
vide Theocritus, i. 15 ; Lucan, iii. 422 ; Philostratus, Heroic. i. art. 4 ; Por-
phyrius de Antro Nymph. c. xxvi. and xxvii.

Held an essentiäl life and a power, as over your members,—
Soothing the rage of the storm by your piteous moans of entreaty,
Staying the impious axe in the paralysed hand of the woodman.
Daphne, tremulous nymph, has fled the benignant asylum
Which, in the shape of the laurel, she found from the heat of
    Apollo ;—
Wan Narcissus has languished away from the languishing
    flower ;—
Hyacinth dwells no more in his brilliant abode, and the stranger
Reads the memorial signs he has left, with a curious pleasure.

Thou art become, oh Echo ! a voice, an inanimate image ;
Where is the palest of maids, dark-tressed, dark-wreathèd with
    ivy,
Who with her lips half-opened, and gazes of beautiful wonder,
Quickly repeated the words that burst on her lonely recesses,
Low in a love-lorn tone, too deep-distracted to answer ?

What must have been thy Nature, oh Greece ! when, marvellous-
    lovely
Now as it is, it is only the tomb of an ancient existence ?

THE RETURN OF ULYSSES.

THE Man of wisdom and endurance rare,
    A sundry-coloured and strange-featured way,
Our hearts have followed ; now the pleasant care
    Is near its end,—the oars' sweet-echoed play,
    Falls on the cliffs of Ithaca's deep bay ;—
The enemy, on whose impetuous breast
    The hero rode undaunted, night and day,
(Such was Minerva's power, and Jove's behest)
Scorns the inglorious strife and lays his wrath to rest.

And how returns the tempest-tossed? his prows
   Gay-garlanded, with grand triumphal song?
Leaps he upon the strand, and proudly vows
   Dire vengeance unto all who did him wrong?
   Not so; for him, all force and passion strong,
And fretful tumult, for a while are o'er,—
   He is borne gently, placidly, along,
And laid upon his own belovèd shore,
Even as a wearied child, in quiet sleep once more!

There is no part of that archaic Lay,
   That strikes with such resistless power on me,
As this pure artist-touch, this tender ray,
   A perfect-simple light of poesy;
   Not the nice wiles of chaste Penelope,—
Not the poor pining dog that died of joy,—
   Not the grey smoke the wande'rer yearned to see,
Whose wavings he had traced, a careless boy,
Sweet as they are, for me this prefer'ence can destroy.

Where the "stone distaffs" of the nymphs of old,
   Still make rich trace'ry in the sacred Cave,—
Where peasants the dark-shadowed Fountain cold,
   Hail by the name the Poet found or gave,
   Where on the Eagle-height the walls out-brave
All time, and only the full-fruited vine
   Trails o'er the home,—it may be o'er the grave,
Of Him for whom these memories combine,—
Rest, care-worn mortal! rest, and let his sleep be thine.

THIÀKE, 1832.

OLYMPUS.

WITH no sharp-sided peak or sudden cone,
  Thou risest o'er the blank Thessalian plain,
But in the semblance of a rounded throne,
  Meet for a monarch and his noble train
  To hold high synod ;—but I feel it vain,
With my heart full and passionate as now,
  To frame my humble verse, as I would fain,
To calm description,—I can only bow
My head and soul, and ask again, "if that be Thou?"

I feel before thee, as of old I felt,
  (With sense, as just, more vivid in degree)
When first I entered, and unconscious knelt
  Within the Roman Martyr's sanctuary :
  I feel that ages laid their faith on Thee,
And if to me thou art a holy hill,
  Let not the Pious scorn,—*that* Piety
Though veiled, *that* Truth, though shadowy, were still
All the world had to raise its heart and fallen will.

Thou Shrine! which man, of his own natural thought,
  Gave to the God of Nature, and girt round
With elemental mightiness, and brought
  Splendour of form and depth of thunde'rous sound,
  To wall about with awe the chosen ground,—
All without toil of slaves or lavished gold,
  Thou wert upbuilt of memories profound,
Imaginations wonderful and old,
And the pure gems that lie in Poets' hearts untold.

God was upon Thee in a thousand forms
  Of Terror and of Beauty, stern and fair,
Upgathered in the majesty of storms,
  Or floating in the film of summer air;
  Thus wert Thou made ideal everywhere;
From Thee the odorous plumes of Love were spread,
  Delight and plenty through all lands to bear,—
From Thee the never-erring bolt was sped
To curb the impious hand or blast the perjured head.

How many a Boy, in his full noon of faith,
  Leaning against the Parthenon, half-blind
With inner light, and holding in his breath,
  Awed by the image of his own high mind,
  Has seen the Goddess there so proudly shrined,
Leave for awhile her loved especial home,
  And pass, though wingless, on the northward wind,
On to thy height, beneath the' eternal dome,
Where Heaven's grand councils wait, 'till Wisdom's self shall
    come.

Ours is another world, and godless now
  Thy ample crown; 'tis well,—yes,—be it so;
But I can weep this moment, when thy brow,
  Light-covered with fresh hoar of autumn snow,
  Shines in white light and chillness, which bestow
New grace of reve'rend loveliness, as seen
  With the long mass of gloomy hills below:
Blest be our open faith! too grand, I ween,
To grudge these votive tears to Beauty that has been.

    LARISA, 1832.

DELPHI.

BENEATH the vintage moon's uncertain light,
   And some faint stars that pierced the film of cloud,
Stood those Parnassian peaks before my sight,
   Whose fame throughout the ancient world was loud.

Still could I dimly trace the terraced lines
   Diverging from the cliffs on either side ;
A theatre whose steps were filled with shrines
   And rich devices of Hellenic pride.

Now brightest daylight would have lit in vain
   The place whence gods and worshippers had fled ;
Only, and they too tenantless, remain
   The hallowed chambers of the pious dead.

Yet those wise architects an ample part
   To Nature gave in their religious shows,
And thus, amid the sepultures of Art,
   Still rise the Rocks and still the Fountain flows.

Desolate Delphi ! pure Castalian spring !
   Hear me avow that I am not as they—
Who deem that all about you ministe'ring
   Were base impostors, and mankind their prey :

That the high names they seemed to love and laud
   Were but the tools their paltry trade to ply ;
This pomp of Faith a mere gigantic fraud,
   The apparatus of a mighty lie !

Let those that will believe it ; I, for one,
  Cannot thus read the history of my kind ;
Remembe'ring all this little Greece has done
  To raise the universal human mind :

I doubt not, hierarchs of that plastic race,
  By faith received and given, could keep alive
Those awful rites and sanctities of place,—
  Believing where they seemed but to contrive :

And thus these mighty sympathies, combined
  With such rare nature as the priestess bore,
Brought to the surface of her stormy mind
  Distracted fragments of prophetic lore.

For, howsoe'er to mortals' probing view
  Creation is revealed, yet must we pause,
Weak to dissect the futile from the true,
  Where vast Imagination spreads her laws.

So now that dimmer grows the watery light,
  And things each moment more fantastic seem,
I fain would seek if still the Gods have might
  Over the undissembling world of dream :

I ask not that for me aside be cast
  The solemn veil that hides what is decreed ;
I crave the resurrection of the past,
  That I may know what Delphi was indeed !

Oct., 1842.

THE TOMB OF LAIUS.

WHERE Delphi's consecrated pass
  Bœotia's misty region faces,*
Rises a tomb-like stony mass
  Amid the bosky mountain-bases ;
It seems no work of human care,
  But many rocks split off from one :
Laius, the Theban king, lies there,—
  His murde'rer Œdipus, his son.

No pilgrim to the Pythian shrine
  But marked the spot with decent awe,
In presence of a power divine,
  O'erruling human will and law :
And to some thoughtful hearts that scene—
  Those paths, that mound, those browsing herds,
Were more than e'er that tale had been,
  Arrayed in Sophoclean words.

So is it yet,—no time or space
  That ancient anguish can assuage,
For sorrow is of every race,
  And suffe'ring due from every age ;
That 'awful legend falls to us,
  With all the weight that Greece could feel,
And every man is Œdipus,
  Whose wounds no mortal skill can heal.

* At the " Schiste Hodos," or " Triodos.

Oh ! call it Providence or Fate,
  The Sphynx propounds the riddle still,
That Man must bear and expiate
  Loads of involuntary ill :
So shall Endurance ever hold
  The foremost rank 'mid human needs,
Not without faith, that God can mould
  To good the dross of evil deeds.

1842.

—————

THE FLOWERS OF HELICON.

THE solitudes of Helicon
  Are rife with gay and scented flowers,
Shining the marble rocks upon,
  Or 'mid the valley's oaken bowers ;
And ever since young Fancy placed
  The Hieron of the Muses here,
Have ceaseless generations graced
  This airy Temple year by year.

But those more bright, more precious, flowers
  With which old Greece the Muses woo'd,
The Art, whose varied forms and powers
  Charmed the poetic multitude,
The Thought, that from each deep recess
  And fissure of the teeming mind
Sent up its odo'rous fruitfulness—
  What have those glories left behind ?

For from those generous calices
  The vegetative virtue shed,
Flew over distant lands and seas,
  Waking wide nations from the dead ;
And e'er the parent plants o'erthrown
  Gave place to rank and noisome weed,
The giant Roman world was sown
  Throughout with that ennobling seed.

And downward thence to latest days
  The heritage of Beauty fell,
And Grecian forms and Grecian lays
  Prolonged their humanising spell,
Till, when new worlds for man to win
  The' Atlantic's riven waves disclose,
The wildernesses there begin
  To blossom with the Grecian rose.

And all this while in barren shame
  Their native land remote reclines,
A mocked and miserable name
  Round which some withered ivy twines :
Where, wandering 'mid the broken tombs,
  The remnant of the race forget
That ever with such royal blooms
  This Garden of the Soul was set.

O breezes of the wealthy West !
  Why bear ye not on grateful wings
The seeds of all your life has blest
  Back to their being's early springs?
Why fill ye not these plains with hopes
  To bear the treasures once they bore,
And to these Heliconian slopes
  Transport civility and lore ?

For now, at least, the soil is free,
  Now that one strong reviving breath
Has chased that Eastern tyranny
  Which to the Greek was ever death :
Now that, though weak with age and wrongs,
  And bent beneath the recent chain,
This motherland of Greece belongs
  To her own western world again.

1842.

MYCENÆ.

I SAW a weird procession glide along
The vestibule before the Lion's gate ;*
A Man of godlike limb and warrior state,
Who never looked behind him, led the throng ;
Next a pale Girl, singing sweet sorrow, met
My eyes, who ever pointed to a fleck
Of ingrained crimson on her marble neck ;
Her a fierce Woman, armed with knife and net,
Close followed, whom a Youth pursued with smile,
Once mild, now bitter-mad, himself the while
Pursued by three foul Shapes, gory and grey :
Dread Family ! . . . I saw another day
The phantom of that Youth, sitting alone,
Quiet, thought-bound, a stone upon a stone.

1832.

* προπύλα τάδι. Elect. 1391.

MARATHON.

I COULD believe that under such a sky,
Thus grave, thus streaked with thunderlight, of yore,
The small Athenian troop rushed onward, more
As Bacchanals, than men about to die.
How weak that massive motley enemy
Seemed to those hearts, full-fed on that high lore,
Which, for their use, in his melodious store,
Old Homer had laid up immortally.
Thus Marathon was Troy,—thus here again,
They were at issue with the barba'rous East,
And favou'ring Gods spoke out, and walked the plain ;
And every man was an anointed priest
Of Nemesis, empowerèd to chastise
The rampant insolence that would not be made wise.

1832.

_____

THERMOPYLÆ.

No parleying with themselves, no pausing thought
　Of worse or better consequence, was there,
Their business was to do what Spartans ought,
　Sparta's chaste honour was their only care.

First in the outlet of that narrowest pass,
　Between the tall straight cliffs and sullen tide,
Before his Faithful, stood Leonidas,—
　Before the Few who could not leave his side.

o

Never the hope of such a precious meed
  Upon his most ambitious dreams had shone,
Through Him the Gods for Sparta had decreed
  More fame than Athens earned at Marathon.

And more than this, he knew in that proud hour,
  How high a price his single Life could claim,
That in its sacrifice there lay the power
  Alone to save his father-land from shame,

Yet was he loth to meet that sacred fate,
  As he there stood, cramped in by rocks and sea,
He would *confront* the Persian myriad's weight,
  And die an unbound Victim, fighting free.

One more fair field,—one last unshackled blow
  Strong with concentrate vengeance, this was all
That still remained to fill to overflow
  The measure of the glory of his fall.

How He, and They who followed him in love,
  Went forth and perished, is a tale to tell,
Such as old Bards to Epic music wove,
  And so felt he who wrote their Chronicle.

The symbol Lion, that once stood in stone
  Over the Lion-hearted, is no more;
Where sat the Last, on their sepulchral throne,
  Is now a thing of antiquarian lore.

Nor mourn for this,—all other truth is vain,
  But this, to know at heart, that They are there,
There in the giant cliffs, and perilous plain,
  Paths, fountains, forest, ocean, every where.

Now let all Thought be Memo'ry,—calmly wait,
  Till clear defined, before thy Spirit's eyes,
Heroic Dignity, impersonate
  In awful phantoms, silently arise.

Between the Men who noble deeds have done,
  And every Poet to the end of time,
There is a brotherly communion,
  One Father-God has made them both sublime :

And thus, to Thee, there can be nothing dead
  Of great things past, they live in thine own will,
Thou givest them form,—they, on thy favoured head,
  Virtues of earth and Heavenly Love distil.

THE CONCENTRATION OF ATHENS.

> " Bards who died content on pleasant sward,
>   Leaving great verse unto a little clan."—KEATS.

WHY should we wonder that from such small space
Of Earth so much of human strength upgrew,
When thus were woven bonds that tighter drew
Round the Athenian heart than faith or race ?
Thus patriotism could each soul imbue
With personal affections, face to face,
And home was felt in every public place,
And brotherhood was never rare or new.
Thus Wisdom, from the neighbouring Parthenon,
Down on the Areopagus could fix
A watchful gaze : thus from the rising Pnyx
The Orator's inspiring voice could reach
Half o'er the City, and his solemn speech
Was as a father's counsel to his son.

PELASGIAN AND CYCLOPEAN WALLS.

YE cliffs of masonry, enormous piles,
Which no rude censure of familiar Time
Nor record of our puny race defiles,
In dateless mystery ye stand sublime,
Memorials of an age of which we see
Only the types in things that once were Ye.

Whether ye rest upon some bosky knoll,
Your feet by ancient myrtles beautified,
Or seem, like fabled dragons, to unroll
Your swarthy grandeurs down a bleak hill-side,
Still on your savage features is a spell
That makes ye half divine, ineffable.

With joy, upon your height I stand alone,
As on a precipice, or lie within
Your shadow wide, or leap from stone to stone,
Pointing my steps with careful discipline,
And think of those grand limbs whose nerve could bear
These masses to their places in mid air ;

Of Anakim, and Titans, and of days
Saturnian, when the spiri't of man was knit
So close to Nature, that his best essays
At Art were but in all to follow it.
In *all*,—dimension, dignity, degree ;
And thus these mighty things were made to be.

VENICE.

"The ruler of the Adriatic, who never was infant nor stripling, whom God took by the right hand and taught to walk by himself the first hour."—LANDOR.

WALK in St. Mark's, the time the ample space
Lies in the freshness of the evening shade,
When, on each side, with gravely darkened face,
The masses rise above the light arcade ;
Walk down the midst with slowly-tunèd pace,
But gay withal,—for there is high parade
Of fair attire and fairer forms, which pass
Like varying groups on a magician's glass.

From broad-illumined chambers far within,
Or under curtains daintily outspread,
Music, and laugh, and talk, the motley din
Of all who from sad thought or toil are sped,
Here a chance hour of social joy to win,
Gush forth,—but *I* love best, above my head
To feel nor arch nor tent, nor anything
But that pure Heaven's eternal covering.

It is one broad Saloon, one gorgeous Hall ;
A chamber, where a multitude, all Kings,
May hold full audience, splendid festival,
Or Piety's most pompous ministerings ;

Thus be its height unmarred,—thus be it all
One mighty room, whose form direct upsprings
To the o'er-arching sky ;—it is right good,
When Art and Nature keep such brotherhood.

For where, upon the firmest sodden land,
Has ever Monarch's power and toil of slaves
Equalled the works of that self-governed band,
Who fixed the Delos of the Adrian waves ;
Planting upon these strips of yielding sand
A Temple of the Beautiful, which braves
The jealous strokes of ocean, nor yet fears
The far more perilous sea, "whose waves are years ?"

Walk in St. Mark's again, some few hours after,
When a bright sleep is on each storied pile,—
When fitful music, and inconstant laughter,
Give place to Nature's silent moonlight smile :
Now Fancy wants no faery gale to waft her
To Magian haunt, or charm-engirded isle,
All too content, in passive bliss, to see
This show divine of visible Poetry :—

On such a night as this impassionedly
The old Venetian sung those verses rare,
"That Venice must of needs eternal be,
For Heaven had looked through the pellucid air,
And cast its reflex in the crystal sea,
And Venice was the image pictured there ;" *
I hear them now, and tremble, for I seem
As treading on an unsubstantial dream.

---

* "Ich hörte einen blinden Sänger in Chioggia, der sang, Venedig sey
eine ewige Stadt ; der Himmel hätte sich im Meer gespiegelt und sein
Widerschein wäre Venedig."—PLATEN.

Who talks of vanished glory, of dead power,
Of things that were, and are not? Is he here?
Can he take in the glory of this hour,
And call it all the decking of a bier?
No, surely as on that Titanic tower *
The Guardian Angel stands in æther clear,
With the moon's silver tempering his gold wing,
So Venice lives, as lives no other thing :—

That strange Cathedral! exquisitely strange,—
That front, on whose bright varied tints the eye
Rests as of gems,—those arches, whose high range
Gives its rich-broidered border to the sky,—
Those ever-prancing steeds !—My friend, whom change
Of restless will has led to lands that lie
Deep in the East, does not thy fancy set
Above those domes an airy minaret?

Dost thou not feel, that in this scene are blent
Wide distances of the estrangèd earth,
Far thoughts, far faiths, beseeming her who bent
The spacious Orient to her simple worth,
Who, in her own young freedom eminent,
Scorning the slaves that shamed their ancient birth,
And feeling what the West could be, had been,
Went out a Trave'ller and returned a Queen?

* The Campanile.

THE VENETIAN SERENADE.

WHEN along the light ripple the far serenade
Has accosted the ear of each passionate maid,
She may open the window that looks on the stream,—
She may smile on her pillow and blend it in dream ;
Half in words, half in music, it pierces the gloom,
" I am coming—Stalì—but you know not for whom !
     Stalì—not for whom ! "

Now the tones become clearer,—you hear more and more
How the water divided returns on the oar,—
Does the prow of the Gondola strike on the stair ?
Do the voices and instruments pause and prepare ?
Oh ! they faint on the ear as the lamp on the view,
" I am passing—Premì—but I stay not for you !
     Premì—not for you ! "

Then return to your couch, you who stifle a tear,
Then awake not, fair sleeper—believe he is here ;
For the young and the loving no sorrow endures,
If to-day be another's, to-morrow is yours ;
May, the next time you listen, your fancy be true.
" I am coming—Sciàr—and for you and to you !
     Sciàr—and to you ! "

The Venetian words here used are the calls of the gondoliers :—
     Stalì—to the right.
     Premì—to the left.
     Sciàr—stop the boat.

A DREAM IN A GONDOLA.

I HAD a dream of waters : I was borne
Fast down the slimy tide
Of eldest Nile, and endless flats forlorn
Stretched out on either side,—
Save where from time to time arose
Red Pyramids, like flames in forced repose,
And Sphynxes gazed, vast countenances bland,
Athwart that river-sea and sea of sand.

It is the nature of the Life of Dream,
To make all action of our mental springs,
Howe'er unnatural, discrepant, and strange,
Be as the' unfolding of most usual things ;
And thus to me no wonder did there seem,
When, by a subtle change,
The heavy, ample, byblus-wingèd, boat,
In which I lay afloat,
Became a deft canoe, light-wove
Of painted bark, gay-set with lustrous shells,
Faintingly rocked within a lonesome cove,
Of some rich island where the Indian dwells ;
Below, the water's pure white light
Took colour from reflected blooms,
And, through the forest's deepening glooms,
Birds of illuminated plumes
Came out like stars in summer-night :
And close beside, all fearless and serene,
Within a niche of drooping green,
A girl, with limbs fine-rounded and clear-brown,
And hair thick-waving down,

Advancing one small foot, in beauty stood,
Trying the temper of the lambent flood.

But on my spirit in that spicèd air
Embalmed, and in luxurious senses drowned,
Another change of sweet and fair
There passed, and of the scene around
Nothing remained the same in sight or sound :
For now the Wanderer of my dream
Was gliding down a fable-stream
Of long-dead Hellas, with much treasure
Of inworking thoughtful pleasure ;
While the silver line meanders
Through the tall pink oleanders,
Through the wood of tufted rushes,
Through the arbute's ruby-bushes,
Voices of a happy hymn
Every moment grow less dim,
Till at last the slim caïque
(Hollowed from a single stem
Of a hill-brow's diadem)
Rests in a deep-dented creek
Myrtle-ambushed,—and above
Songs, the very breath of Love,
Stream from Temples reverend-old,
Porticoes of Doric mould,
Snow-white islands of devotion,
Planted in the rose and gold
Of the evening's æther-ocean ;—
O joyant earth ! belovèd Grecian sky !
O favoured Wanderer—honoured dreamer I !

Yet not less favoured when awake,—for now,
Across my torpid brow

Swept a cool current of the young night's air,
With a sharp kiss, and there
Was I all clear awake,—drawn soft along
There in my own dear Gondola, among
The bright-eyed Venice isles,
Lit up in constant smiles.—
What had my thoughts and heart to do
With wild Egyptian bark, or frail canoe,
Or mythic skiff out of Saturnian days,
When I was there, with that rare scene to praise,
That Gondola to rest in and enjoy,
That actual bliss to taste without alloy?

Cradler of placid pleasures, deep delights,
Bosomer of the Poet's wearied mind,
Tempter from vulgar passions, scorns and spites,
Enfolder of all feelings that be kind!
Before our souls thy quiet motions spread,
In one great calm, one undivided plain,
Immediate joy, blest memories of the dead,
And iris-tinted forms of hope's domain,
Child of the still Lagoons!
Open to every show
Of summer sunsets and autumnal moons,
Such as no other space of world can know,—
Dear Boat! that makest dear
Whatever thou com'st near,—
In thy repose still let me gently roam,
Still on thy couch of beauty find a home;
Still let me share thy comfortable peace
With all I have of dearest upon Earth,
Friend, mistress, sister; and when death's release
Shall call my spirit to another birth,

Would that I might thus lightly lapse away,
Alone,—by moonlight,—in a Gondola.

―――――

AT ·VENICE.

Not only through the golden haze
Of indistinct surprise,
With which the Ocean-bride displays
Her pomp to stranger eyes ;—
Not with the fancy's flashing play,   ,
The trave'ller's vulgar theme,
Where following objects chase away
The moment's dazzling dream ;—

Not thus art thou content to see
The City of my love,—
Whose beauty is a thought to me
All mortal thoughts above ;
And pass in dull unseemly haste,
Nor sight nor spirit clear,
As if the first bewilde'ring taste
Were all the banquet here !

When the proud Sea, for Venice' sake,
Itself consents to wear
The semblance of a land-locked lake,
Inviolably fair ;
And in the dalliance of her Isles,
Has levelled his strong waves,
Adoring her with tende'rer wiles,
Than his own pearly caves,—

Surely may *we* to simi'lar calm
Our noisy lives subdue,
And bare our bosoms to such balm
As God has given to few :
Surely may we delight to pause
On our care-goaded road,
Refuged from Time's most bitter laws
In this august abode.

Thou knowest this,—thou lingerest here,
Rejoicing to remain ;
The plashing oars fall on thy ear
Like a familiar strain ;
No wheel prolongs its weary roll,
The Earth itself goes round
Slower than elsewhere, and thy soul
Dreams in the void of sound.

Thy heart, by Nature's discipline,
From all disdain refined,
Kept open to be written in
By good of every kind,
Can harmonise its inmost sense
To every outward tone,
And bring to all experience
High reasoning of its own.

So, when these forms come freely out,
And wonder is gone by,
With patient skill it sets about
Its subtle work of joy ;

Connecting all it comprehends
By lofty moods of love,—
The earthly Present's farthest ends,—
The Past's deep Heaven above.

O bliss! to watch, with half-shut lid,
By many a secret place,
Where darkling loveliness is hid,
And undistinguished grace,—
To mark the gloom, by slow degrees,
Exfoliate, till the whole   .
Shines forth before our sympathies,
A soul that meets a soul!

Come out upon the broad Lagoon,
Come for the hundredth time,—
Our thoughts shall make a pleasant tune,
Our words a worthy rhyme;
And thickly round us we will set
Such visions as were seen,
By Tizian and by Tintorett,
And dear old Giambellin,—

And all their peers in art, whose eyes,
Taught by this sun and sea,
Flashed on their works those burning dyes,
That fervent poetry;
And wove the shades so thinly-clear
They would be parts of light
In northern climes, where frowns severe
Mar half the charms of sight.—

Did ever shape that Paolo drew
Put on such brilliant tire,
As Nature, in this evening view,—
This world of tinted fire?
The glory into whose embrace,
The virgin pants to rise,
Is but reflected from the face
Of these Venetian skies.

The sun, beneath the horizon's brow
Has sunk, not passed away ;
His presence is far lordlier now
Than on the throne of day ;
His spirit of splendour has gone forth,
Sloping wide violet rays,
Possessing air and sea and earth
With his essential blaze. *

Transpierced, transfused, each densest mass
Melts to as pure a glow,
As images on painted glass
Or silken screens can show.
Gaze on the city,—contemplate
With that fine sense of thine
The Palace of the ancient state,—
That wildly-grand design !

---

* The perfect transparency and rich colour of all objects, and their
reflections, in southern countries, for some short time after sunset, has an
almost miraculous effect to a northern eye. Whenever it has been imi-
tated in art, it has been generally pronounced unnatural or exaggerated.
I do not remember to have ever seen the phenomenon so astonishingly
beautiful as at Venice, at least in Italy.

How 'mid the universal sheen
Of marble amber-tinged,
Like some enormous baldaquin
Gay-chequered and deep-fringed,
It stands in air and will not move,
Upheld by magic power,—
The dun-lead Domes just caught above—
Beside,—the glooming Tower.

Now a more distant beauty fills
Thy scope of ear and eye,—
That graceful cluster of low hills,
Bounding the western sky,
Which the ripe evening flushes cover
With purplest fruitage bloom,—
Methinks that gold-lipt cloud may hover
Just over Petrarch's tomb !

Petrarch ! when we that name repeat,
Its music seems to fall
Like distant bells, soft-voiced and sweet,
But sorrowful withal ;—
That broken heart of love !—that life
Of tenderness and tears !
So weak on earth,—in earthly strife,—
So strong in holier spheres !

How in his most of godlike pride,
While emu'lous nations ran
To kiss his feet, he stept aside
And wept the woes of man !

How in his genius-woven bower
Of passion ever green,
The world's black veil fell, hour by hour,
Him and his rest between.

Welcome such thoughts ;—they well atone
With this more serious mood
Of visible things that night brings on,
In her cool shade to brood ;
The moon is clear in heaven and sea,
Her silver has been long
Slow-changing to bright gold, but she
Deserves a separate song.

ODE

TO THE MOON OF THE SOUTH.

LET him go down,—the gallant Sun !
  His work is nobly done ;
  Well may He now absorb
  Within his solid orb
The rays so beautiful and strong,
The rays that have been out so long
Embracing this delighted land as with a mystic song.

Let the brave Sun go down to his repose,
  And though his heart be kind,
  He need not mourn for those
    He leaves behind ;
He knows, that when his ardent throne
Is rolled beyond the vaulting sky,
The Earth shall not be left alone
In darkness and perplexity.

We shall not sit in sullen sorrow
Expectant of a tardy morrow,
But there where he himself arose,
    Another power shall rise,
And gracious rivalry disclose
    To our reverted eyes,
Between the passing splendour and the born,
Which can the most our happy world adorn.

   The light of night shall rise,—
Not as in northern skies,
A memo'ry of the day, a dream
Of sunshine, something that might seem
Between a shadow and a gleam,
A mystery, a maiden
Whose spirit worn and sorrow laden
Pleasant imaginations wile
Into a visionary smile,
A novice veiled in vapoury shrouds,
A timid huntress, whom the clouds
    Rather pursue than shun,—
    With far another mien,
    Wilt Thou come forth serene,
    Thou full and perfect Queen,
Moon of the South! twin-sister of the Sun!

Still harboured in his tent of cloth of gold
He seems thy ordered presence to await,
In his pure soul rejoicing to behold
The majesty of his successor's state,—
    Saluting thy ascent
With many a tender and triumphant tone
Compassed in his celestial instrument,
And harmonies of hue to other climes unknown.

He too, who knows what melody of word
May with that visual music best accord,
Why does the Bard his homage now delay?
  As in the ancient East,
  The royal Minstrel-Priest
Sang to his harp that Hallelujah lay
Of the Sun-bridegroom ready for his way,
So, in the regions of the later West
  This blessed even-tide,
Is there no Poet whose divine behest
  Shall be to hail the bride?

A feeble voice may give an earnest sound,
And grateful hearts are measured not by power,
Therefore may I, tho' nameless and uncrowned,
Proffer a friendly tribute to thy dower.
For on the midland Sea I sailed of old,
Leading thy line of narrow rippled light,
And saw it grow a field of frosted gold,
With every boat a Shadow in the Bright;
And many a playful fancy has been mine,
As I have watched the shapes thy glory made,
Glimpsing like starlight through the massive pine,
Or finely-trellised by mimosa shade;
And now I trace each moment of thy spell,
That frees from mortal stain these Venice isles,
From eve's rich shield to morn's translucid shell,
From Love's young glow to Love's expiring smiles!

We gaze upon the faces we hold dear,
Each feature in thy rays as well defined,
As just a symbol of informing mind,
As when the noon is on them full and clear;

Yet all some wise attempered and subdued,
Not far from what to Faith's prospective eyes
Transfigured creatures of beatitude
    From earthy graves arise.

Those evenings, oh ! those evenings, when with one,
Then the world's loveliness, now wholly mine,
I stood beside the salient founts that shone
Fit frontispiece to Peter's Roman shrine ;
I knew how fair were She and They
In every bright device of day,
All happy as a lark on wing,
A singing, glistening, dancing thing,
With joy and grace that seemed to be
Of Nature's pure necessity ;
But when, O holy Moon ! thy might
Turned all the water into light,
And each enchanted Fountain wore
Diviner beauty than before,
A pillar of aspiring beams,
An ever-falling veil of gleams,—
She who in day's most lively hour
Had something of composing power
About her mirthful lips and eyes,—
Sweet folly making others wise,—
Was vested with a sudden sense
Of great and grave intelligence,
As if in thy reflex she saw
The process of eternal law,
God's conscious pleasure working out
Through all the Passion, Pain, and Doubt ;—
And thus did She and Thou impart
Such knowledge to my listening heart,

Such sympathies as word or pen
    Can never tell again !

All spirits find themselves fulfilled in Thee,
The glad have triumph and the mourning balm :
Dear God ! how wondrous that a thing should be
So very glorious and so very calm !
The lover, standing on a lonely height,
Rests his sad gaze upon the scene below,
Lapt in the trance of thy pervading glow,
Till pleasant tears obscure his pensive sight ;
And in his bosom those long-smothered flames,
The scorching elements of vain desire,
Taking the nature of thy gentle fire,
Play round the heart in peace, while he exclaims,
" Surely my Love is out somewhere to-night ! "

Why art thou thus companionable ?   Why
Do we not love thy light alone, but Thee ?
Is it that though thou art so pure and high,
Thou dost not shock our senses, as they be ?
That our poor eyes rest on thee, and descry
Islands of earth within thy golden sea ?
    Or should the root be sought
    In some unconscious thought,
That thy fine presence is not more thine own
Than are our soul's adorning splendours ours ?— '
    Than are the energies and powers,
    With which reflected light alone
    Illuminates the living hours,
    From our own wells of being brought,
From virtue self-infused or seed of life self-sown ?
Thus with ascent more ready may we pass
From this delightful sharing of thy gifts

Up to the common Giver, Source, and Will ;
              And if, alas !
His daily-affluent sun-light seldom lifts
To thankful ecstasy our hearts' dull mass,
        It may be that our feeble sight
        Will not confront the total light,
        That we may love, in nature frail,
        To blend the vivid with the pale,
            The dazzling with the dim :
        And lo ! how God, all-gracious still
        Our simplest fancies to fulfil,
Bids us, O Southern Moon, thy beauty hail,
In Thee rejoicing and adoring Him.

SIR WALTER SCOTT AT THE TOMB OF THE STUARTS.*

EVE's tinted shadows slowly fill the fane
Where Art has taken almost Nature's room,
While still two objects clear in light remain,
An alien pilgrim at an alien tomb.—

—A sculptured tomb of regal heads discrown'd,
Of one heart-worshipped, fancy-haunted, name,
Once loud on earth, but now scarce else renown'd
Than as the offspring of that stranger's fame.

* When Sir Walter Scott was at Rome, the year of his death, the history and localities of the Stuarts seemed to absorb all other objects of his interest. The circumstance of this poem fell within the observation of the writer.

There lie the Stuarts !—There lingers Walter Scott !
Strange congress of illustrious thoughts and things !
A plain old moral, still too oft forgot,—
The power of Genius and the fall of Kings.

The curse on lawless Will high-planted there,
A beacon to the world, shines not for him ;
He is with those who felt their life was sere,
When the full light of loyalty grew dim.

He rests his chin upon a sturdy staff,
Historic as that sceptre, theirs no more ;
His gaze is fixed ; his thirsty heart can quaff,
For a short hour the spirit-draughts of yore.

Each figure in its pictured place is seen,
Each fancied shape his actual vision fills,
From the long-pining, death-delivered, Queen,
To the worn Outlaw of the heathe'ry hills.

O grace of life, which shame could never mar !
O dignity, that circumstance defied !
Pure is the neck that wears the deathly scar,
And sorrow has baptised the front of pride.

But purpled mantle, and blood-crimson'd shroud,
Exiles to suffer and returns tó woo,
Are gone, like dreams by daylight disallow'd ;
And their historian,—he is sinking too !

A few more moments and that labou'ring brow
Cold as those royal busts and calm will lie ;
And, as on them his thoughts are resting now,
His marbled form will meet the attentive eye.

Thus, face to face, the dying and the dead,
Bound in one solemn ever-living bond,
Communed ; and I was sad that ancient head
Ever should pass those holy walls beyond.

———

THE ILLUMINATIONS OF ST. PETER'S.

I.

FIRST ILLUMINATION.

TEMPLE ! where Time has wed Eternity,
How beautiful Thou art, beyond compare,
Now emptied of thy massive majesty,
And made so faery-frail, so faery-fair :
The lineaments that thou art wont to wear
Augustly traced in ponderous masonry,
Lie faint as in a woof of filmy air,
Within their frames of mellow jewelry.—
But yet how sweet the hardly-waking sense,
That when the strength of hours has quenched those gems,
Disparted all those soft-bright diadems,—
Still in the Sun thy form will rise supreme
In its own solid clear magnificence,
Divinest substance then, as now divinest dream.

———

II.

SECOND ILLUMINATION.

MY heart was resting with a peaceful gaze,
So peaceful that it seemed I well could die
Entranced before such Beauty,—when a cry
Burst from me, and I sunk in dumb amaze :

The molten stars before a withering blaze
Paled to annihilation, and my eye,
Stunned by the splendour, saw against the sky
Nothing but light,—sheer light,—and light's own haze.
At last that giddying Sight took form,—and then
Appeared the stable Vision of a Crown,
From the black vault by unseen Power let down,
Cross-topped,—thrice girt with flame :—

　　　　　　　　　　　　　　　　Cities of men,
Queens of the Earth ! bow low,—was ever brow
Of mortal birth adorned as Rome is now ?

———

III.

REFLECTION.

PAST is the first dear phantom of our sight,
A loadstar of calm loveliness to draw
All souls from out this world of fault and flaw,
To a most perfect centre of delight,
Merged in deep fire ;—our joy is turned to awe,
Delight to wonder.　This is just and right ;—
A greater light puts out the lesser light,—
So be it ever,—such is God's high law.
The self-same Sun that calls the flowers from earth
Withers them soon, to give the fruit free birth ;—
The nobler Spirit to whom much is given
Must take still more, though in that more there lie
The risk of losing All ;—to gaze at Heaven,
We blind our earthly eyes ;—to live we die.

THE FIREWORKS

FROM THE CASTLE OF ST. ANGELO.

PLAY on, play on, I share your gorgeous glee,
Creatures of elemental mirth ! play on,—
Let each fulfil his marvellous destiny,
My heart leaps up and falls in unison.
The Tower round which ye weave, with elfin grace,
The modulations of your burning dance,
Looks through your gambols with a grandsire's face,
A grave but not reproachful countenance ;
Ye are the children of a festive night,
He is the mate of many an hundred years,—
Ye but attest men's innocent delight,
He is the comrade of their crimes and tears,—
Ye in your joys' pure prime will flare away,
He waits his end in still and slow decay.

———

ON THE

MARRIAGE OF THE LADY GWENDOLIN TALBOT

WITH THE

ELDEST SON OF THE PRINCE BORGHESE.

LADY ! to decorate thy marriage-morn,
Rare gems, and flowers, and lofty songs are brought ;
Thou the plain utter'ance of a Poet's thought,
Thyself at heart a Poet, wilt not scorn :

The name, into whose splendour thou wert born,
Thou art about to change for that which stands
Writ on the proudest work * that mortal hands
Have raised from earth, Religion to adorn.
Take it rejoicing,—take with thee thy dower,
Britain's best blood, and Beauty ever new,
Being of mind ; may the cool northern dew
Still rest upon thy leaves, transplanted flower !
Mingling thy English nature, pure and true,
With the bright growth of each Italian hour.

ROME, May 11th, 1835.

ON THE DEATH OF THE PRINCESS BORGHESE,

AT ROME, NOVEMBER, 1840.

ONCE, and but once again I dare to raise
A voice which thou in spirit still may'st hear,
Now that thy bridal bed becomes a bier,
Now that thou canst not blush at thine own praise !
The ways of God are not as our best ways,
And thus we ask, with a convulsive tear,
Why is this northern blossom low and sere ?
Why has it blest the south but these few days ?
Another Basilic,† decked otherwise
Than that which hailed thee as a princely bride,
Receives thee and three little ones beside ;
While the young lord of that late glorious home
Stands 'mid these ruins and these agonies,
Like some lone column of his native Rome !

* St. Peter's.
† S. Maria Maggiore, where the Borghese family are interred.

NAPLES AND VENICE.

OVERLOOKING, overhearing, Naples and her subject bay,
Stands Camaldoli, the convent, shaded from the' inclement ray.

Thou, who to that lofty terrace lov'st on summer-eve to go,
Tell me, Poet! what Thou seest, what Thou hearest, there
below!

Beauty, beauty, perfect beauty! Sea and City, Hills and Air,
Rather blest imaginations than realities of fair.

Forms of grace alike contenting casual glance and stedfast gaze,
Tender lights of pearl and opal mingling with the diamond
blaze.

Sea is but as deepen'd æther: white as snow-wreaths sunbeshone
Lean the Palaces and Temples green and purple heights upon.

Streets and paths mine eye is tracing, all replete with clamo'rous
throng,
Where I see, and where I see not, waves of uproar roll along.

As the sense of bees unnumber'd, burning through the walk of
limes,—
As the thought of armies gathe'ring round a chief in ancient
times,—

So from Corso, Port, and Garden, rises Life's tumultuous strain,
Not secure from wildest utter'ance rests the perfect-crystal main.

Still the all-enclosing Beauty keeps my spirit free from harm,
Distance blends the veriest discords into some melodious charm.

—OVERLOOKING, overhearing, Venice and her sister isles,
Stands the giant Campanile massive 'mid a thousand piles.

Thou who to this open summit lov'st at every hour to go,
Tell me, Poet! what Thou seest, what Thou hearest, there
    below.

Wonder, wonder, perfect wonder! Ocean is the City's moat;
On the bosom of broad Ocean seems the mighty weight to
    float :

Seems—yet stands as strong and stable as on land e'er city
    shall,—
Only moves that Ocean-serpent, tide-impelled, the Great Canal.

Rich arcades and statued pillars, gleaming banners, burnished
    domes,—
Ships approaching,—ships departing,—countless ships in har-
    bour-homes.

Yet so silent! scarce a murmur winged to reach this airy seat,
Hardly from the close Piazza rises sound of voice or feet.

Plash of oar or single laughter,—cry or song of Gondolier,—
Signals far between to tell me that the work of life is here.

Like a glorious maiden dreaming music in the drowsy heat,
Lies the City, unbetokening where its myriad pulses beat.

And I think myself in cloudland,—almost try my power of will,
Whether I can change the picture, or it must be Venice still.

When the question wakes within me, which hath won the
    crown of deed,
Venice with her moveless silence, Naples with her noisy speed ?

Which hath writ the goodlier tablet for the past to hoard and
    show,
Venice in her student stillness, Naples in her living glow?

Here are Chronicles with virtues studded as the night with
    stars,—
Records there of passions raging through a wilderness of wars :

There a tumult of Ambitions, Power afloat on blood and tears,—
Here one simple reign of Wisdom stretching thirteen hundred
    years :

Self-subsisting, self-devoted, there the moment's Hero ruled,—
Here the State, each one subduing, pride enchained and passion
    schooled :

Here was Art the nation's mistress, Art of colour, Art of stone—
There before the leman Pleasure bowed the people's soul alone.

Venice ! vocal is thy silence, can our soul but rightly hear ;
Naples ! dumb as death thy voices, listen we however near.

SWITZERLAND AND ITALY.

WITHIN the Switzer's varied land,
When Summer chases high the snow,
You'll meet with many a youthful band
Of strangers wandering to and fro :

Through hamlet, town, and healing bath,
They haste and rest as chance may call,
No day without its mountain-path,
No path without its waterfall.

They make the hours themselves repay,
However well or ill be shared,
Content that they should wing their way,
Unchecked, unreckoned, uncompared :
For though the hills unshapely rise,
And lie the colours poorly bright,—
They mould them by their cheerful eyes,
And paint them with their spirit's light.

Strong in their youthfulness, they use
The energies their souls possess ;
And if some wayward scene refuse
To pay its part of loveliness,—
Onward they pass, nor less enjoy
For what they leave ;—and far from me
Be every thought that would destroy
A charm of that simplicity !

But if *one* blot on that white page
From Doubt or Mise'ry's pen be thrown,—
If *once* the sense awake, that Age
Is counted not by years alone,—
Then no more grand and wondrous things !
No active happinesses more !
The wounded Heart has lost its wings,
And change can only fret the sore.

Yet there is calm for those that weep,
Where the divine Italian sea
Rests like a maiden hushed asleep
And breathing low and measuredly ;
Where all the sunset-purpled ground,
Fashioned by those delicious airs,
Seems strewed with softest cushions round
For weary heads to loose their cares :

Where Nature offers, at all hours,
Out of her free imperial store,
That perfect Beauty their weak powers
Can help her to create no more :
And grateful for that ancient aid,
Comes forth to comfort and relieve
Those minds in prostrate sorrow laid,
Bidding them open and receive !

Though still 'tis hardly she that gives,
For Nature reigns not there alone,
A mightier queen beside her lives,
Whom she can serve but not dethrone ;
For she is fallen from the state
That waited on her Eden-prime,
And Art remains by Sin and Fate
Unscathed, for Art is not of Time.

ON

THE CHURCH OF THE MADELEINE, AT PARIS.

I.

THE Attic temple whose majestic room
Contained the presence of Olympian Jove,
With smooth Hymettus round it and above,
Softe'ning the splendour by a sober bloom,
Is yielding fast to Time's irreverent doom ;
While on the then barbarian banks of Seine
That nobler type is realised again
In perfect form, and dedicate—to whom ?
To a poor Syrian girl, of lowliest name,
A hapless creature, pitiful and frail
As ever wore her life in sin and shame,—
Of whom all histo'ry has this single tale,—
" She loved the Christ, she wept beside his grave,
And He, for that Love's sake, all else forgave."

II.

If one, with prescient soul to understand
The working of this world beyond the day
Of his small life, had taken by the hand
That wanton daughter of old Magdala ;
And told her that the time was ripe to come
When she, thus base among the base, should be
More served than all the Gods of Greece and Rome,
More honoured in her holy memory,—

Q

How would not men have mocked and she have scorned
The fond Diviner ?—Plausible excuse
Had been for them, all moulded to one use
Of feeling and of thought, but We are warned
By such ensamples to distrust the sense
Of Custom proud and bold Experience.

———

III.

Thanks to that element of heavenly things,
That did come down to earth, and there confound
Most sacred thoughts with names of usual sound,
And homeliest life with all a Poet sings.
The proud Ideas that had ruled and bound
Our moral nature were no longer kings,
Old Power grew faint and shed his eagle-wings,
And grey Philosophy was half uncrowned.
Love, Pleasure's child, betrothed himself to Pain ;—
Weakness, and Poverty, and Self-disdain,
And tranquil sufferance of repeated wrongs,
Became adorable ;—Fame gave her tongues,
And Faith her hearts to objects all as low
As this lorn child of infamy and woe.

———

FRANCE AND ENGLAND.

O France and England ! on whose lofty crests
The day-spring of the Future flows so free,
Save where the cloud of your hostility
Settles between and holy light arrests,
Shall Ye, first instruments of God's behests,
But blunt each other ? Shall Barbarians see
The two fair sisters of civility
Turn a fierce wrath against each other's breasts ?

No !—by our common hope and being—no !
By the expanding might and bliss of peace,
By the revealed insanity of war,
England and France shall not be foe to foe :
For how can earth her store of good increase,
If what God loves to make man's passions still will mar ?

ON MILTON'S COTTAGE,

AT CHALFONT ST. GILES,

Where he remained during the Great Plague.

BENEATH this roof, for no such use designed
By its old owners, Fleetwood's banished race,
Blind Milton found a healthful resting-place,
Leaving the city's dark disease behind :—
Here, too, with studies noble and refined,
As with fresh air, his spirits he could brace,
And grow unconscious of the time's disgrace,
And the fierce plague of disappointed mind.
The gracious Muse is wont to build for most
Of her dear sons some pleasant noontide bower ;
But for this One she raised a home of fame,
Where he dwelt safe through life's chill evening hour,
Above the memo'ry of his Hero lost,
His martyred brethren and his country's shame.

ANSWER TO WORDSWORTH'S SONNET AGAINST THE KENDAL AND BOWNESS RAILWAY.

THE hour may come, nay must in these our days,
When the swift steam-car with the cata'ract's shout
Shall mingle its harsh roll, and motley rout
Of multitudes these mountain echoes raise.

But Thou, the Patriarch of these beauteous ways,
Canst never grudge that gloomy streets send out
The crowded sons of labour, care, and doubt,
To read these scenes by light of thine own lays.
Disordered laughter and encounters rude
The Poet's finer sense perchance may pain,
But many a glade and nook of solitude
For quiet walk and thought will still remain,
Where He those poor intruders can elude,
Nor lose one dream for all their homely gain.

TINTERN ABBEY.

The Men who called their passion piety,
And wrecked this noble argosy of faith,—
They little thought how beauteous could be Death,
How fair the face of Time's aye-deepe'ning sea !
Nor arms that desolate, nor years that flee,
Nor hearts that fail, can utterly deflower
This grassy floor of sacramental power,
Where we now stand commu'nicants—even We,
We of this latter, still protéstant age,
With priestly ministrations of the Sun
And Moon and multitudinous quire of stars
Maintain this consecration, and assuage
With tender thoughts the past of weary wars,
Masking with good that ill which cannot be undone.

ON THE GRAVE OF BISHOP KEN,

AT FROME, IN SOMERSETSHIRE.

LET other thoughts, where'er I roam,
  Ne'er from my memory cancel
The coffin-fashioned tomb at Frome
  That lies behind the chancel;
A basket-work where bars are bent,
  Iron in place of osier,
And shapes above that represent
  A mitre and a crosier.

These signs of him that slumbers there
  The dignity betoken;
These iron bars a heart declare
  Hard bent but never broken;
This form pourtrays how souls like his, .
  Their pride and passion quelling,
Preferr'd to earth's high palaces
  This calm and narrow dwelling.

There with the church-yard's common dust
  He loved his own to mingle;
The faith in which he placed his trust
  Was nothing rare or single;
Yet laid he to the sacred wall
  As close as he was able,
The blessèd crumbs might almost fall
  Upon him from God's table.

Who was this Father of the Church,
　So secret in his glory?
In vain might antiquarians search
　For record of his story;
But preciously tradition keeps
　The fame of holy men;
So there the Christian smiles or weeps
　For love of Bishop Ken.

A name his country once forsook,
　But now with joy inherits,
Confessor in the Church's book,
　And Martyr in the Spirit's!
That dared with royal power to cope,
　In peaceful faith persisting,
A braver Becket—who could hope
　To conquer unresisting!

POEMS.

LEGENDARY AND HISTORICAL.

A CHRISTMAS STORY.

THE windows and the garden door
Must now be closed for night,
And you, my little girl, no more
Can watch the snow-flakes white
Fall, like a silver net, before
The face of dying light.

Draw down the curtains every fold,
Let not a gap let in the cold,
Bring your low seat toward the fire,
And you shall have your heart's desire ;
A story of that favou'rite book
In which you often steal a look,
Regretful not to understand
Words of a distant time and land ;—
That small square book that seems so old
In tawny white and faded gold,
And which I could not leave to-day,
Even with the snow and you to play.—
It was on such a night as this,,
  Six hundred years ago,
The wind as loud and pitiless,
  As loaded with the snow,

A night when you might start to meet
A friend in an accustomed street,
That a lone child went up and down
The pathways of an ancient town.
A little child, just such as you,
With eyes, though clouded, just as blue,
With just such long fine golden hair,
But wet and rough for want of care,
And just such tender totte'ring feet
Bare to the cold and stony street.

Alone! this fragile human flower,
Alone! at this unsightly hour,
A playful, joyful, peaceful form,
　A creature of delight,
Become companion of the storm,
　. And phantom of the night!
No gentler thing is near,—in vain
Its warm tears meet the frozen rain,
No watchful ears await its cries
On every name that well supplies
The childly nature with a sense
Of love and care and confidence;
It looks before, it looks behind,
And staggers with the weighty wind,
Till, terror overpowering grief,
And feeble as an autumn leaf,
It passes down the tide of air,
It knows not, thinks not, how or where.

Beneath a carven porch, before
An iron-belted oaken door,
The tempest drives the cowe'ring child,
And rages on as hard and wild.

This is not shelter, though the sleet
Strikes heavier in the open street,
For, to that infant ear, a din
Of festive merriment within
Comes, by the contrast, sadder far
Than all the outer windy war,
With something cruel, something curst,
In each repeated laughter-burst ;
A thread of constant cheerful light,
Drawn through the crevice on the sight,
Tells it of heat it cannot feel,
   And all the fire-side bliss
That home's dear portals can reveal
   On such a night as this.
How can those hands so small and frail,
Empassioned as they will, avail
Against that banded wall of wood
Standing in senseless hardihood
Between the warmth and love and mirth,
The comforts of the living earth,
And the lorn creature shivering there,
The plaything of the savage air ?

We would not, of our own good will,
Believe in so much strength of ill,
Believe that life and sense are given
To any being under Heaven
Only to weep and suffer thus,
   To suffer without sin
What would be for the worst of us
   A bitter discipline.
Yet now the tiny hands no more
Are striking that unfeeling door ;

Folded and quietly they rest,
As on a cherub's marble breast ;
And from the guileless lips of woe
Are passing words confused and low,
Remembered fragments of a prayer,
Learned and repeated otherwhere,
With the blue summer overhead,
  On a sweet mother's knee,
Beside the downy cradle-bed,
  But always happily.

Though for those holy words the storm
Relaxes not its angry form,
The child no longer stands alone
Upon the inhospitable stone :
There now are two,—one to the other
Like as a brother to twin-brother,
But the new-comer has an air
Of something wonderful and rare,
Something divinely calm and mild,
Something beyond a human child ;
His eyes come through the thicke'ning night
With a soft planetary light,
And from his hair there falls below
A radiance on the drifting snow,
And his untarnished childly bloom
Seems but the brighter for the gloom.

See what a smile of gentle grace
Expatiates slowly o'er his face !
As, with a mien of soft command,
He takes that numbed and squalid hand,
And with a voice of simple joy
And greeting as from boy to boy,

He speaks, " What do you at this door?
Why called you not on me before?
What like you best? that I should break
This sturdy barrier for your sake,
And let you in that you may share
The warmth and joy and cheerful fare ;—
Or will you trust to me alone,
And heeding not the windy moan
Nor the cold rain nor lightning-brand,
Go forward with me, hand in hand?
Within this house, if e'er on earth,
You will find love and peace and mirth ;
And there may rest for many a day,
While I am on mine open way ;
And should your heart to me incline,
   When I am gone,
Take you this little cross of mine
   To lean upon,
And setting out what path you will,
Careless of your own strength and skill,
You soon will find me ; only say,
What wish you most to do to-day?"
The child looks out into the night,
With gaze of pain and pale affright,
Then turns an eye of keen desire
On the thin gleam of inward fire,
Then rests a long and silent while,
Upon that brother's glorious smile.
—You've seen the subtle magnet draw
The iron by its hidden law,
So seems that smile to lure along
The child from an enclosing throng
Of fears and fancies undefined,
And to one passion fix its mind,—

Till every struggling doubt to check
   And give to love its due,
It casts its arms about his neck,
   And cries " With You, with You,—
For you have sung me many a song,
Like mine own mother's, all night long,
And you have play'd with me in dreams,
Along the walks, beside the streams,
Of Paradise,—the blessèd bowers,
Where what men call the stars are flowers,
And what to them looks deep and blue
Is but a veil which we saw through,
Into the garden without end,
Where you the angel-children tend :
So that they asked me when I woke,
Where I had been, to whom I spoke,
What I was doing there, to seem
So heavenly-happy in my dream ?

Oh ! take me, take me, there again,
Out of the cold and wind and rain,
Out of this dark and cruel town,
Whose houses on the orphan frown ;
Bear me the thundering clouds above
To the safe kingdom of your love :
Or if you will not, I can go
With you barefooted through the snow ;—
I shall not feel the bitter blast,
If you will take me home at last."

Three kisses on its dead-cold cheeks,—
Three on its bloodless brow,—
And a clear answe'ring music speaks,
" Sweet brother ! come there now :

It shall be so; there is no dread
Within the aureole of mine head;
This hand in yours, this living hand,
Can all the world of cold withstand,
And, though so small, is strong to lift
Your feet above the thickest drift;
The wind that round you raged and broke
Shall fold about us like a cloak,
And we shall reach that garden soon,
Without the guide of sun or moon."
So down the mansion's slippe'ry stair,
   Into the midnight weather,
Pass, as if sorrows never were,
   The weak and strong together.

—This was the night before the morn,
On which the Hope of Man was born,
And long ere dawn can claim the sky,
The tempest rolls subservient by;
While bells on all sides sing and say,
How Christ the child was born to-day;
Free as the sun's in June, the rays
Mix merry with the Yuhl-log's blaze;
Some butterflies of snow may float
Down slowly, gliste'ning in the mote,
But crystal-leaved and fruited trees
Scarce lose a jewel in the breeze;
Frost-diamonds twinkle on the grass,
   Transformed from pearly dew,
And silver flowers encrust the glass,
   Which gardens never knew.

The inmates of the house, before
Whose iron-fended heedless door,

The children of our nightly tale
Were standing, rise refreshed and hale,
And run, as if a race to win,
To let the Christmas morning in.
They find, upon the threshold stone,
A little Child, just like their own ;
Asleep it seems, but when the head
Is raised, it sleeps, as sleep the dead ;
The fatal point had touched it, while
The lips had just begun a smile,
The forehead 'mid the matted tresses
A perfect-painless end expresses,
And, unconvulsed, the hands may wear
The posture more of thanks than prayer.

They tend it straight in wondering grief,—
And, when all skill brings no relief,
They bear it onward, in its smile,
Up the Cathedral's central aisle :
There, soon as Priests and People heard
How the thing was, they speak not word,
But take the usual Image, meant
The blessèd babe to represent,
Forth from its cradle, and instead
Lay down that silent mortal head.
Now incense-cloud and anthem-sound
Arise the beauteous body round ;
Softly the carol chant is sung,
Softly the mirthful peal is rung,
And, when the solemn duties end,
With tapers earnest troops attend
The gentle corpse, nor cease to sing
    Till, by an almond tree,
They bury 'it, that the flowers of spring
    May o'er it soonest be.

PRINCE EMILIUS OF HESSEN-DARMSTADT.

FROM Hessen-Darmstadt every step to Moskwa's blazing banks
Was Prince Emilius found in fight before the foremost ranks;
And when upon the icy waste that host was backward cast,
On Beresina's bloody bridge his banner waved the last.

His valour shed victorious grace on all that dread retreat,
That path across the wilde'ring snow, athwart the blinding sleet;
And every follower of his sword could all endure and dare,
Becoming warriors strong in hope or stronger in despair.

Now, day and dark, along the storm the demon Cossacks
        sweep,
The hungriest must not look for food, the weariest must not
        sleep;
No rest, but death, for horse or man, whichever first shall
        tire;—
They see the flames destroy but ne'er may feel the saving fire.

Thus never closed the bitter night nor rose the savage morn,
But from that gallant company some noble part was shorn,
And, sick at heart, the Prince resolved to keep his purposed way,
With stedfast forward looks, nor count the losses of the day.

At length beside a black-burnt hut, an island of the snow,—
Each head in frigid stupor bent toward the saddle-bow,—
They paused, and of that sturdy troop, that thousand banded
        men,
At one unmeditated glance he numbered only ten !

Of all that high triumphant life that left his German home,
Of all those hearts that beat beloved or looked for love to come,
This piteous remnant hardly saved his spirit overcame,
While memory raised each friendly face and called each ancient
    name.

Then were his words serene and firm—"Dear brothers it is
    best
That here, with perfect trust in Heaven, we give our bodies
    rest ;
If we have borne, like faithful men, our part of toil and pain,
Where'er we wake, for Christ's good sake, we shall not sleep in
    vain."

Some murmured, others looked, assent, they had no heart to
    speak;
Dumb hands were pressed, the pallid lips approached the callous
    cheek ;
They laid them side by side ; and death to him at least did
    seem
To come attired in mazy robe of variegated dream.

Once more he floated on the breast of old familiar Rhine,
His mother's and one other smile above him seemed to shine ;
A blessèd dew of healing fell on every aching limb,
Till the stream broadened and the air thickened and all was
    dim.

Nature had bent to other laws, if that tremendous night
Passed o'er his frame exposed and worn and left no deadly
    blight ;
Then wonder not that when refreshed and warm he woke at
    last,
There lay a boundless gulf of thought between him and the past.

Soon raising his astonished head he found himself alone,
Sheltered beneath a genial heap of vestments not his own ;
The light increased, the solemn truth revealing more and
       more,—
His soldiers corses self-despoiled closed up the narrow door.

That very hour, fulfilling good, miracu'lous succour came,
And Prince Emilius lived to give this worthy deed to fame.
O brave fidelity in death !   O strength of loving will !
These are the holy balsam-drops that woful wars distil.

THE TRAGEDY OF THE LAC DE GAUBE IN THE PYRENEES.

THE marrriage-blessing on their brows,
Across the Channel seas
And lands of gay Garonne, they reach
The pleasant Pyrenees :—
He into boyhood born again,
A son of joy and life,—
And she a happy English girl,
A happier English wife.

They loiter not where Argelés,
The chesnut-crested plain,
Unfolds its robe of green and gold
In pasture, grape, and grain ;
But on and up, where Nature's heart
Beats strong amid the hills,
They pause, contented with the wealth
That either bosom fills.

R

There is a Lake, a small round Lake,
High on the mountain's breast,
The child of rains and melted snows,
The torrent's summer rest,—
A mirror where the vete'ran rocks
May glass their peaks and scars,
A nether sky where breezes break
The sunlight into stars.

Oh ! gaily shone that little lake,
And Nature, sternly fair,
Put on a sparkling countenance
To greet that merry pair ;
How light from stone to stone they leapt,
How trippingly they ran ;
To scale the rock and gain the marge
Was all a moment's span !

" See, dearest, this primæval boat,
So quaint, and rough, I deem
Just such an one did Charon ply
Across the Stygian stream :
Step in,—I will your Charon be,
And you a Spirit bold,—
I was a famous rower once
In college days of old.

" The clumsy oar ! the laggard boat !
How slow we move along,—
The work is harder than I thought,—
A song, my love, a song !"

Then, standing up, she carolled out
So blithe and sweet a strain
That the long-silent cliffs were glad
To peal it back again.

He, tranced in joy, the oar laid down,
And rose in careless pride,
And swayed in cadence to the song
The boat from side to side :
Then clasping hand in loving hand,
They danced a childish round,
And felt as safe in that mid-lake
As on the firmest ground.

One poise too much !—He headlong fell.—
She stretching out to save
A feeble arm, was borne adown
Within that glitte'ring grave :—
One moment, and the gush went forth
Of music-mingled laughter,—
The struggling splash and deathly shriek
Were there the instant after.

Her weaker head above the flood,
That quick engulfed the strong,
Like some enchanted water flower,
Waved pitifully long :—
Long seemed the low and lonely wail
Athwart the tide to fade ;
Alas ! that there were some to hear,
But never one to aid.

Yet not alas ! if Heaven revered
The freshly-spoken vow,
And willed that what was then made one
Should not be sundered now ;
If She was spared, by that sharp stroke,
Love's most unnatu'ral doom,
The future lorn and unconsoled,
The unavoided tomb !

But weep, ye very Rocks ! for those,
Who, on their native shore,
Await the letters of dear news,
That shall arrive no more ;
One letter from a stranger hand,—
Few words are all the need,—
And then the fune'ral of the heart,
The course of useless speed !

The presence of the cold dead wood,
The single mark and sign
Of her so loved and beautiful,
That handiwork divine !
The weary search for his fine form
That in the depth would linger,
And late success,—Oh ! leave the ring
Upon that faithful finger.

And if in life there lie the seed
Of real enduring being,
If love and truth be not decreed
To perish unforeseeing ;

This Youth, the seal of death has stamped,
No time can wither never,
This Hope, that sorrow might have damped,
Is fresh and strong for ever. *

THE PERSECUTION OF THE TEMPLARS.

THE towe'ring cliffs of Gavarnie,
Severely closing round
My onward steps, had seemed to me
A nation's natural bound :
The topmost ridge with cloud was bent,
Save where antique Rolànd
Is said the mountain to have rent
With his gigantic hand.

The hazy memo'ry of the Knight
Of Faery suited well
The huge dimensions of that sight,
And touched them with his spell ;
I almost saw the armour glance
In every chance sun-ray,
And feathers move and horses prance
Amid the cata'ract-spray.

When swift within me rose the thought
Of some chiválrous forms,
Who bodily here dwelt and fought
With worse than Nature's storms ;

* Mr. and Mrs. Patteson were drowned in the year 1831.

Some hunters of these vales and hills
Who stood, themselves, at bay
Against the fierce pursuit that kills
The honour of its prey :—

The Soldier-monks, whose quaint old Church
I left at Luz, time-worn,
Whose records Histo'ry loves to search,
And searches but to mourn :
The Warriors of the sacred Grave,
Who looked to Christ for laws,
And perished for the faith they gave
Their Comrades and the Cause.

They perished, in one fate alike,
The vete'ran and the boy,
Where'er the regal arm could strike
To torture and destroy ;
While darkly, down the stream of time,
Devised by evil fame,
Float murmurs of mysterious crime
And tales of secret shame.

How oft when ava'rice, hate, or pride
Assault some noble band,
The outer world, (that scorns the side
It does not understand,)
Echoes each foul derisive word,
Gilds o'er each hideous sight,
And consecrates the wicked sword
With names of holy Right !

Yet, by these lessons, men awake,
To know they cannot bind
Discordant will in one, and make
An aggregate of mind ;
For e'en should hearts and hands combine
In one expressive whole,
Still brutal force can burst the line
And dissipate the soul.

For, ever, in our best essays
At close fraternal ties,
An evil narrowness waylays
Our purest sympathies ;
And love, however bright it burn
For what it holds most fond,
Is tainted by its unconcern
For all that lies beyond.

Wider—oh ! wider every hour,
While mortal sight is blind,
Vibrates the circle of the power
That sanctifies mankind ;
Wider—oh ! wider, undulate
Emotions, that impart
To man the grandeur of his fate
The glory of his heart,

And still the earth has many a knight,
By high vocation bound
To conquer in enduring fight
The Spirit's Holy Ground ;

And manhood's pride and hopes of youth
Still meet the Templars' doom,—
Crusaders of the' ascended Truth,
Not of the empty Tomb!

·

———

·

THE BEGGAR'S CASTLE.

A STORY OF THE SOUTH OF FRANCE.

THOSE ruins took my thoughts away
   To a far eastern land;
Like camels in a herd, they lay
   Upon the dull red sand;
I know not that I ever sate
Within a place so desolate.

Unlike the relics that connect
   Our hearts with ancient Time,
All moss-besprent and ivy-deckt,
   Gracing a lenient clime,
Here all was death and nothing born,—
No life but the unfriendly thorn.

"My little guide, whose sunny eyes
   And darkly-lucid skin,
Witness, in spite of shrouded skies,
   Where southern realms begin;
Come, tell me all you 've heard and know
About these mighty things laid low."

The " Beggar's Castle," wayward name,
  Was all these fragments bore,
And wherefore legendary fame
  Baptised them thus of yore,
He told in words so sweet and true,
I wish that he could tell it you.

A puissant Seigneur, who in wars
  And tournays had renown,
With wealth from prudent ancestors
  Sloping unbroken down,
Dwelt in these towers, and held in fee
All the broad lands that eye can see.

He never tempered to the poor
  Misfortune's bitter blast,
And when before his haughty door
  Widow and orphan past,
Injurious words and dogs at bay
Were all the welcome that had they.

The Monk who toiled from place to place,
  That God might have his dole,
Was met by scorn and foul grimace,
  And oaths that pierced his soul ;
'T was well for him to flee and pray,
" They know not what they do and say."

One evening, when both plain and wood
  Were trackless in the snow,
A Beggar at the portal stood,
  Who little seemed to know
That Castle and its evil fame,
As if from distant shores he came.

Like channeled granite was his front,
  His hair was crisp with rime,—
He asked admittance, as was wont
  In that free-hearted time ;
For who would leave to die i' the cold
A lonely man and awful-old.

At first his prayer had no reply,—
  Perchance the wild wind checked it,
But when it rose into a cry,
  No more the inmates recked it,
Till where the cheerful fire-light shone,
A voice out-thundered,—" Wretch ! begone."

" There is no path,—I have no strength,—
  What can I do alone ?
Grant shelter, or I lay my length,
  And perish on the stone ;
I crave not much,—I should be blest
In kennel or in barn to rest."

" What matters thy vile head to me ?
  Dare not to touch the door ! "
" Alas ! and shall I never see
  Home, wife, and children more ? "—
" If thou art still importunate,
My serfs shall nail thee to the gate."

But, when the wrathful Seigneur faced
  The object of his ire,
The beggar raised his brow debased
  And armed his eyes with fire :
" Whatever guise is on me now,
I am a mightier Lord than thou ! "

"Madman or cheat! announce thy birth."—
  " *That* thou wilt know to-morrow."
"Where are thy fiefs?"—"The whole wide Earth."
  "And what thy title?"—"SORROW."
Then, opening wide his ragged vest,
He cried,—"Thou canst not shun thy guest."

He stamped his foot with fearful din,—
  With imprecating hand
He struck the door, and past within
  Right through the menial band:
"Follow him, seize him,—There—and there!"
They only saw the blank night air.

But He was at his work: ere day,
  Began the work of doom,
The Lord's one daughter, that fair may,
  Fled with a base-born groom,
Bearing about, where'er she came,
The blighting of an ancient name.

His single son,—that second self,
  Who, when his first should fall,
Would hold his lands and hoarded pelf,
  Died in a drunken brawl;—
And now alone amidst his gold
He stood, and *felt* his heart was cold.

Till, like a large and patient sea
  Once roused by cruel weather,
Came by the raging Jacquerie,
  And swept away together
Him and all his, save that which time
Has hoarded to suggest our rhyme.

THE BROWNIE.

A GENTLE household Spirit, unchallenged and unpaid,
Attended with his service a lonely servant-maid.

She seemed a weary woman, who had found life unkind,
Whose youth had left her early and little left behind.

Most desolate and dreary her days went on until
Arose this unseen stranger her labours to fulfil.

But now she walked at leisure, secure of blame she slept,
The meal was always ready, the room was always swept.

And, by the cheerful fire-light, the winter evenings long,
He gave her words of kindness and snatches of sweet song ;—

With useful housewife secrets and tales of faeries fair,
From times when gaunt magicians and dwarfs and giants were.—

Thus, habit closing round her, by slow degrees she nurst
A sense of trust and pleasure, where she had feared at first.

When strange desire came on her, and shook her like a storm,
To see this faithful being distinct in outward form.

He was so pure a nature, of so benign a will,
It could be nothing fearful, it could be nothing ill.

At first with grave denial her prayer he laid aside,
Then warning and entreaty, but all in vain, he tried.

The wish upgrew to passion,—she urged him more and more,—
Until, as one outwearied, but still lamenting sore,

He promised in her chamber he would attend her call,
When from the small high window the full-moon light should
       fall.

Most proud and glad that evening she entered to behold
How there her phantom Lover his presence would unfold ;

When lo ! in bloody pallor lay, on the moonlit floor,
The Babe she bore and murdered some thirteen years before.,

BERTRAND DU GUESCLIN.

A BRETON BALLAD.

I.

'TWAS on the field of Navarrète,
When Trestamare had sought
From English arms a safe retreat,
Du Guesclin stood and fought:
And to the brave Black Prince alone
He yielded up his sword ;—
So we must sing in mournful tone,
Until it be restored ;—

CHORUS.

Spin, spin, maidens of Brittany,
    And let not your Litany
    Come to an end,
    Before you have prayed
    The Virgin to aid
Bertrand du Guesclin, our Hero and Friend.

II.

The Black Prince is a gentle knight ;
And bade Du Guesclin name
What ransom would be fit and right
For his renown and fame ;
" A question hard,"—says he, " yet since
Hard Fortune on me frowns,
I could not tell you less, good Prince,
Than twenty thousand crowns."

III.

" Where find you all that gold, Sir Knight?
I would not have you end
Your days in sloth and undelight
Away from home and friend : "
" O Prince of gene'rous heart and just !
Let all your fears be stayed ;
For' my twenty thousand crowns I trust
To every Breton maid."

IV.

And he is not deceived, for we
Will never let him pine
In stranger towers beyond the sea,
Like' a jewel in the mine !
No work but this shall be begun,—
We will not rest or dream,
Till twenty thousand crowns are spun
Du Guesclin to redeem.

V.

The Bride shall grudge the marriage morn,
And feel her joy a crime ;

The mother' shall wean her eldest-born
A month before its time ;
No festal day shall idle by,
No hour uncounted stand,
The grandame in her bed shall die
With' the spindle in her hand.

CHORUS.

Spin, spin, women of Brittany,
Nor let your Litany
Come to an end,
Before you have prayed
The Virgin to aid
Bertrand du Guesclin, our Hero and Friend.

THE FALL OF ALIPIUS. *

WHEN gentle Gratian ruled the Roman west,
And with unvigo'rous virtues thought to hold
That troubled balance in perpetual rest,
And crush with good intent the bad and bold,
The youth Alipius for the first time saw
The Mother of civility and law.

Mother in truth, but yet as one who now
By her disloyal children tended ill
Should sit apart, with hand upon her brow,
Moaning her sick desires and feeble will ;
So Rome was pictured to the subtler eye,
That could through words the soul of things descry.

* Suggested by the Confessions of St. Augustin.

But no such vision of the truth had He
Who with full heart passed under the old wall,
A Roman moulded by that sun and sea
Which lit and laved the infant Hannibal.
One who with Afric blood could still combine
The civic memo'ries of a Roman line.

To him was Rome whatever she had been,
Republican, Cesarean, unforgot,
As much the single undisputed Queen,
As if the Empire of the East was not,—
Fine gold and rugged iron fused and cast
Into one image of the glorious Past:

And on a present throne to heaven up-piled,
Of arches, temples, basilics and halls,
He placed his Idol, while before her filed
Nations to gild and glut her festivals ;
And of her might the uttera'nce was so loud,
That every other living voice was cowed.

Possessed by this idea, little heed
At first he gave the thicke'ning multitude,
That met and passed him in their noisy speed,
Like hounds intent upon the scent of blood,
For all the City was that day astir,
Tow'ard the huge Flavian Amphitheatre.

Yet soon his sole attention grew to scan
That edifice whose walls might rather seem
The masonry of Nature than of man,
In size and figure a Titanic dream,
That could whole worlds of lesser men absorb
Within the' embrace of one enormous orb.

The mighty tragedies of skill and strife,
That there in earnest death must ever close,
Exciting palates which no tastes of life
Could to a sense of such delight dispose,
Swept by his fancy with an hundred names,
The pomps and pageantries of Roman games.

Why should he not pass onward with that tide
Of passionate enchantment? why not share
The seeds of pleasure Nature spread so wide,
And gave the heart of men like common air?
Why should that be to him a shame and sin,
Which thousands of his fellows joy'd to win?

But ere this thought could take perspicuous form,
His Will arose and fell'd it at a blow;
For he had felt that instinct's fever-storm
Lash his young blood to fury long ago,—
And in the Circus had consumed away
Of his best years how many' a wanton day!

Till the celestial guardian of his soul
Led him the great Augustin's voice to hear,
And soon that better influence o'er him stole,
A reve'rend master and companion dear,
From whom he learnt in his provincial home
Wisdom scarce utter'd in the schools of Rome:

" How wide Humanity's potential range,—
From Earth's abysses to serenest Heaven,—
From the poor child of circumstance and change,
By every wind of passion tossed and driven,
To the established philosophic mind,
The type and model of the thing designed:

s

"And how this work of works in each is wrought,
By no enthusiast leap to good from ill,
But by the vigo'rous government of thought,
The unrelaxing continence of will,—
Where little habits their invis'ible sway
Extend, like body's growth, from day to day."

By meditations such as these sustained
He stoutly breasted that on-coming crowd,
Then, as in stupor, at one spot remained,
For thrice he heard his name repeated loud,
And close before him there beheld in truth
Three dearest comrades of his Afric youth.

O joy ! to welcome in a stranger land
Our homeliest native look and native speech,
To feel that in one pressure of the hand
There is a world of sympathy for each ;
And if old friendliness be there beside,
The meeting is of bridegroom and of bride.

What questions asked that waited not reply !
What mirthful comment on apparent change !
Till the three raised one gratulating cry,—
"Arrived just then ! how fortunate,—how strange !
Arrived to see what they ne'er saw before,
The fight between the Daunian and the Moor.

"One graceful-limbed and lofty as a palm,
The other moulded like his mountain-pine ;
Each with his customed arms content and calm,
In his own nation each of princely line,—
Two natures sepa'rate as the sun and snow
Battling to death to make a Roman show ! "—

—Alipius, with few words and earnest mien,
Answered, " That he long since had stood apart
From those ferocious pleasures, and would wean
Those whom he loved from them with all his heart,
Yet, as his counsel could have little power,
Where should they meet the morrow,—at what hour? ".

Their shafts of mock'ery from his virtuous head
Fell to the ground,—so, using ruder might,
Amid applauding bystanders, they said,
" They would divert him in his own despite,"
And bore him forward, while in fearless tone
He cried, "my mind and sight are still mine own."

His body a mere dead-weight in their hands,
His angry eyes in proud endurance closed,
They placed him where spectators from all lands
In eager expectation sat disposed,
While in the distance still, before, behind,
The people gathering were as rushing wind :

Which ever rising grew into a storm
Of acclamations, when, at either end,
The combatant displayed his perfect form,
Brandished his arms, rejoicing to expend
His life in fight at least,—at least reclaim
A warrior's privilege from a captive's shame.

As rose before Amphion's notes serene
The fated City of heroic guilt,
Alipius thus his soul and sense between
Imagination's strong defence up-built,
With soft memorial music, dreamy strains
Of youthful happinesses, loves, and pains.

S 2

His stony seat seems on the Libyan coast,—
Augustin on one side, and on the other
Monica, for herself beloved, yet most
By him regarded as Augustin's mother;
And from far off resounds the populous roar
As but the billows booming on the shore.

Never can He desert the truth he drew
From those all-honoured lips,—never can yield
To savage appetite, and fresh imbrue
That soul in filth to which had been revealed
The' eternal purities that round it lie,
The Godhead of its birth and destiny.

—Now trumpets clanging forth the last command
Gave place to one tremendous pause of sound,
Silence like that of some rich-flowe'ring land
With lava-torrents raging underground,
Scarce for one moment safe from such outbreak
As shall all nature to its centre shake.

And soon in truth it came ;—the first sharp blows
Fell at long intervals as aimed with skill,
Then grew expressive of the passion-throes
That followed calm resolve and prudent will,—
Till wild ejaculations took their part
In the death-strife of hand and eye and heart.

" Habet,—Hoc habet,—Habet ! "* What a cry!
As if the Circus were one mighty mouth
Invading the deep vale of quiet sky
With ava'lanche melted in the summer-drouth,—
Arti'culate tumult from old earth upborne,
Delight and ire and ecstasy and scorn !

       * He is hit—he has got it !

Sat then Alipius silent there alone,
With fast-shut eyes and spirit far away?
Remained he there as stone upon the stone,
While the flushed conqu'eror asked the sign to slay
The stricken victim, who despairing dumb
Waited the sentence of the downward thumb?

The shock was too much for him—too, too strong
For that poor Reason and self-resting Pride;
And every evil fury that had long
Lain crouching in his breast leaped up and cried
" Yield, yield at once, and do as others do,
We are the Lords of all of them and you."

The Love of contest and the Lust of blood
Dwell in the depths of man's origi'nal heart,
And at mere shows and names of wise and good
Will not from their barbaric homes depart,
But half asleep await their time, and then
Bound forth, like tigers from their jungle-den :

And all the curious wicker-work of thought,
Of logical result and learned skill,
Of precepts with examples inter-wrought,
Of high ideals, and determinate will,—
The careful fabric of ten thousand hours,
Is crushed beneath the moment's brutal powers.

Thus fell Alipius! He, so grave and mild,
Added the bloody sanction of his hand
To the swift slaughter of that brother-child
Of his own distant Mauritanian land,
Seeming content his very life to merge
In the confusion of that foaming surge.

The rage subsided ; the deep sandy floor
Sucked the hot blood ; the hook, like some vile prey,
Dragged off the noble body of the Moor ;
The Victor, doomed to die some other day,
Enjoyed the plaudits purposelessly earned,—
And back Alipius to himself returned.

There is a fearful waking unto woes,
When sleep arrests her charitable course,
Yet far more terrible the line that flows
From ebrious passion to supine remorse ;
Then welcome death,—but that the suffe'rers feel
Wounds such as theirs no death is sure to heal !

But the demoniac power that well can use
Self-trust and Pride as instruments of ill,
Can such prostration to its ends abuse,
And poison from Humility distil :
" Why struggle more ?   Why strive, when strife is vain,
—An infant's muscles with a giant's chain ? "

So in his own esteem debased, and glad
To take distraction whencesoe'er it came,
Though in his heart of hearts entirely sad,
Alipius lived to pleasure and to fame : *
Sometimes remindful of his youth's high vow,
Of hopes and aspirations, fables now.

When came to Rome his sire of moral lore,
That Master, whom his love could ne'er forget,
He too a proud Philosopher no more,
He too his past reviewing with regret,
But preaching One, who can on man bestow
Truth to be wise and strength to keep him so.

* Alipius was appointed Assessor of Justice to the Treasurer of Italy.

The secret of that strength the Christian sage
To his regained disciple there unsealed,
Giving his stagnant soul a war to wage
With weapons that at once were sword and shield ;
And thenceforth ever down Tradition glide
Augustin and Alipius side by side.*

And in this strength years afterward arose
That aged priest Telemachus, who cast
His life among those brutalising shows,
And died a willing victim and the last,
Leaving that temple of colossal crime
In silent battle with almighty Time.

CHARLEMAGNE, AND THE HYMN OF CHRIST.

"And when they had sung an hymn, they went out into the mount of Olives."—MATT. XXVI. 30 ; MARK XIV. 26.

THE great King Karl sat in his secret room,—
   He had sat there all day ;
He had not called on minstrel knight or groom
   To wile one hour away.

Of arms or royal toil he had no care,
   Nor e'en of royal mirth ;
As if a poor lone monk he rather were,
   Than lord of half the earth.

* They went together to Milan, where they were both baptised by St. Ambrose on Easter Eve, A.D. 387. Thence they returned to Africa, and lived in monastic community in their native town of Tagaste. Alipius afterwards removed to Hippo, and visited St. Jerome in Palestine : he was consecrated Bishop of Tagaste, A.D. 393.

But chance he had some pleasant company,
  Dear wife, familiar friend,
With whom to let the quiet hours slip by,
  As if they had no end ?

The learnèd Alcuin, that large-browed clerk,
  Was there within, and none beside ;
A book they read, and, where the sense was dark,
  He was a trusty guide.

What book had worth so long to occupy
  The thought of such a king,
To make the weight of all that sovere'ignty
  Be a forgotten thing ?

Surely it were no other than the one,
  Whose every line is fraught
With what a mightier King than He had done,
  Conquered, endured, and taught.

There his great soul, drawn onward by the eye,
  Saw in plain chronicle portrayed
The slow unfolding of the mystery
  On which its life was stayed.

There read he how when Jesus, our dear Lord,
  To men of sin and dust had given,
By the transforming magic of his word,
  The bread of very Heaven ;

So that our race, by Adam's fatal food
  Reduced to base decline,
Partaking of that body and that blood,
  Might be again divine,—

After this wondrous largess, and before
   The unimagined pain,
Which, in Gethsemane, the Saviour bore
   Within his heart and brain,—

He read, how these two acts of Love between,
   Ere that prolific day was dim,
Christ and his Saints, like men with minds serene,
   Together sung a hymn.

These things he read in childly faith sincere,
   Then paused and fixed his eye,
And said with kingly utte'rance—" I must hear
   That Hymn before I die.

" I will send forth through sea and sun and snows,
   To lands of every tongue,
To try if there be not some one which knows
   The music Jesus sung.

" For I have found delight in songs profane
   Trolled by a foolish boy,
And when the monks intone a pious strain,
   My heart is strong in joy ;

" How blessèd then to hear those harmonies,
   Which Christ's own voice divine engaged !
'Twould be as if a wind from Paradise
   A wounded soul assuaged."

Within the Empe'ror's mind that anxious thought
   Lay travailing all night long,
He dreamed that Magi to his hand had brought
   The burthen of the Song ;

And when to his grave offices he rose,
  He kept his earnest will,
To offer untold guerdons unto those
  Who should that dream fulfil.

But first he called to counsel in the hall
  Wise priests of reve'rend name,
And with an open counte'nance to them all
  Declared his hope and aim.

He said, "It is God's pleasure, that my will
  Is made the natural law
Of many nations, so that out of ill
  All good things I may draw.

"Therefore this holy mission I decree,
  Sparing no pains or cost,
That thus those sounds of dearest memory
  Be not for ever lost."

They spake. "Tradition streameth thro' our race,
  Most like the gentle whistling air,
To which of old Elias veiled his face,
  Conscious that God was there:

"Not in the storm, the earthquake, and the flame,
  That troubled Horeb's brow,
The splendour and the power of God then came,
  Nor thus he cometh now.

"The silent water filtereth through earth,
  One day to bless the summer land;
The Word of God in Man slow bubbleth forth,
  Touched by a worthy hand.

" Thus, in the memo'ry of some careful Jew
  May lurk the record of a tune
Wont to be sung in ceremonial due
  After the Paschal noon ;

" And thy deep yearning for this mystic song
  May give mankind at last
Some charm and blessing that has slept full long
  The slumber of the Past."

The King rejoiced, and, at this high behest,
  Men, to all toil and change inured,
Passed out to search the World if East or West
  That legend still endured.

What good or ill those venturous hearts befell,
  What glory or what shame,—
How far they wandered, I have not to tell ;
  Each has his sepa'rate fame.

I only know, that when the weight of hours
  The prime of mortal heads had bowed,
He, slowly letting go his outward powers,
  Spoke from his couch aloud :—

" My soul has waited many a linge'ring year
  To taste that one delight,
And now I know at last that I shall hear
  The hymn of Christ to-night.

" Look out, good friends ! be prompt to welcome home,
  Straight to my presence bring,
My messengers, who hither furnished come
  The Song of Christ to sing."

Dark sank that night, but darker rose the morn,
 That found the western earth
Of the divinest presence stripped and shorn
 It ever woke to birth.

It seemed beyond the common lawful sway
 Of Death and Nature o'er our kind,
That such a one as He should pass away,
 And aught be left behind.

In Aachen Abbey's consecrated ground,
 Within the hollowed stone,
They placed the imperial body, robed and crowned,
 Seated as on a throne.

While the blest spirit holds communion free
 With that eternal quire,
Of which on earth to trace the memory
 Was his devout desire. *

---

* It is probable that the hymn sung on this occasion was the Hallèl,
or part of it. The Hallèl is invariably chanted in all Jewish families on
the two first evenings of the Passover, and consists of Psalms 113, 114,
115, 116, 117, and 118, and is also read in the synagogue on every day
of that feast.

THE NORTHERN KNIGHT IN ITALY.*

THIS is the record, true as his own word,
Of the adventures of a Christian knight,
Who, when beneath the foul Karasmian sword †
God's rescued city sunk to hopeless night,
Desired, before he gain'd his northern home,
To soothe his wounded heart at holy Rome.

And having found, in that reflected heaven,
More than Cæsarean splendors and delights,
So that it seemed to his young sense was given
An unimagined world of sounds and sights ;—
Yet, half regretful of the long delay,
He joined some comrades on their common way.

The Spring was mantling that Italian land,
The Spring ! the passion-season of our earth,
The joy, whose wings will never all expand,—
The gladsome travail of continuous birth,—
The force that leaves no creature unimbued
With amorous Nature's bland inquietude.

Though those hard sons of tumult and bold life,
Little as might be, own'd the tender power,
And only show'd their words and gestures rife
With the benign excitement of the hour,—
Yet one, the one of whom this tale is told,
In his deep soul was utterly controll'd.

---

* The story of Tannhäuser is now so well known through Mr. Julian
Fane's and other Poems, that it is unnecessary to repeat the historical
notice of former editions : " Der Tannhäuser und Ewige Jude " of Grüsse
(Dresden, 1861) gives the whole cycle of the Legend.

† At the conclusion of the last crusade.

New thoughts sprung up within him,—new desires
Opened their panting bosoms to the sun :
Imagination scattered lights and fires
O'er realms before impenetrably dun ;
His senses, energized with wondrous might,
Mingled in lusty contest of delight.

The once-inspiring talk of steel and steeds
And famous captains lost its ancient zest ;
The free recital of illustrious deeds
Came to him vapid as a thrice-told jest ;
His fancy was of angels penance-bound
To convoy sprites of ill through heavenly ground.

The first-love vision of those azure eyes,
Twin stars that blessed and kept his spirit cool,
Down-beaming from the brazen Syrian skies,
Now seem'd the spectral doting of a fool,—
Unwelcome visitants that stood between
Him and the livelier glories of the scene.

What wanted he with such cold monitors ?
What business had he with the past at all ?
Well, in the pauses of those clamo'rous wars,
Such dull endearment might his heart enthral,
But, in this universe of blissful calm,
He had no pain to need that homely balm.

Occasion, therefore, in itself though slight
He made of moment to demand his stay,
Where some rare houses, in the clear white light,
Like flakes of snow among the verdure lay ;
And bade the company give little heed,
He would o'ertake them by redoubled speed.

But now at length resolved to satisfy
The appetite of beauty, and repair
Those torpid years which he had let glide by,
Unconscious of the powers of earth and air,
He rested, roved, and rested while he quafft
The deepest richness of the sunny draught.

Eve after eve he told his trusty band
They should advance straight northward on the morrow,
Yet when he rose, and to that living land
Addressed his farewell benison of sorrow,
With loveliest aspect Nature answer'd so,
It seem'd almost impiety to go.

Thus days were gather'd into months, and there
He linger'd, saunte'ring without aim or end :
Not unaccompanied ; for wheresoe'er
His steps, through wood, or glen, or field, might tend,—
A bird-like voice was ever in his ear,
Divinely sweet and rapturously clear.*

From the pinaster's solemn-tented crown,—
From the fine olive spray that cuts the sky,—
From bare or flowering summit, floated down
That music unembodied to the eye :
Sometimes beside his feet it seemed to run,
Or fainted, lark-like, in the radiant sun.

---

* A bird is by no means an uncommon actor in a drama of this kind. It is recorded that, at the Council of Basle, three pious doctors were wont to walk out daily and discuss points of deep theology, but that, as soon as the song of a certain nightingale reached their ears, their argument was inevitably confused ; they contradicted themselves, drew false conclusions, and were occasionally very near falling into heresy. The thought struck one of them to exorcise the nightingale, and the devil flew visibly out of a bush, and left the disputants at peace. See also the beautiful story of "The Monk and Bird," in Dean Trench's poems.

Soon as this mystic sound attained his ear,
Barriers arose, impermeable, between
Him and the two wide worlds of hope and fear ;—
His life entire was in the present scene ;
The passage of each day he only knew
By the broad shadows and the deepening blue.

His senses by such ecstasy possest,
He chanced to climb a torrent's slippery side,
And, on the utmost ridge refusing rest,
Took the first path his eager look descried ;
And paused, as one outstartled from a trance,
Within a place of strange significance.

A ruin'd temple of the Pagan world,—
Pillars and pedestals with rocks confused,—
Art back into the lap of nature hurl'd,
And still most beautiful, when most abused ;
A paradise of pity, that might move
Most careless hearts, unknowingly, to love !

A very garden of luxurious weeds,
Hemlock in trees, acanthine leaves outspread,
Flowers here and there, the growth of wind-cast seeds,
With vine and ivy draperies overhead ;
And by the access, two nigh-sapless shells,
Old trunks of myrtle, haggard sentinels !

Amid this strife of vigour and decay .
An Idol stood, complete, without a stain,
Hid by a broad projection from the sway
Of winter gusts and daily-rotting rain.
Time and his agents seem'd alike to spare
A thing so unimaginably fair.

By what deep memo'ry or what subtler mean
Was it, that at the moment of this sight,
The actual past—the statue and the scene,
Stood out before him in historic light?
He knew the glorious image by its name—
Venus! the Goddess of unholy fame.

He heard the tread of distant generations
Slowly defiling to their place of doom:
And thought how men, and families, and nations
Had trusted in the endless bliss and bloom
Of Her who stood in desolation there,
Now lorn of love and unrevered by prayer.

Beauty without an eye to gaze on it,
Passion without a breast to lean upon,
Feelings unjust, unseemly, and unfit,
Troubled his spirit's high and happy tone;
So back with vague imaginative pain
He turned the steps that soon returned again.

For there henceforth he eve'ry noon reposed
In languor self-sufficient for the day,
Feeling the light within his eyelids closed,
Or peeping, where the locust, like a ray,
Shot through its crevice, and, without a sound,
The insect host enjoyed their airy round.

Day-dreams give sleep, and sleep brings dreams anew;
Thus oft a face of untold tenderness,
A cloud of woe with beauty glistening through,
Brooded above him in divine distress,—
And sometimes bowed so low, as it would try
His ready lips, then vanished with a sigh:

T

And round him flowed through that intense sunshine
Music, whose notes at once were words and tears ;
" Paphos was mine, and Amathus was mine,
Mine were the' Idalian groves of ancient years,—
The happy heart of Man was all mine own,
Now I am homeless and alone—alone ! "

At other times, to his long-resting gaze,
Instinct with life the solid sculpture grew,
And rose transfigured, 'mid a golden haze,
Till lost within the' impermeable blue ;
Yet ever, though with liveliest hues composed,
Sad-swooning sounds the apparition closed.

As the strong waters fill the leaky boat
And suck it downwards, by unseen degrees :—
So sunk his soul, the while it seemed to float
On that serene security of ease,
Into a torpid meditative void,
By the same fancies that before upbuoyed.

His train, though wonde'ring at their changeful lord,
Had no distaste that season to beguile
With mimic contests and well-furnished board,—
And even he would sometimes join awhile
Their sports, then turn, as if in scorn, away
From such rude commerce and ignoble play.

One closing eve, thus issuing forth, he cried,
" Land of my love ! in thee I cast my lot ;—
Till death thy faithful subject I abide,—
Home, kindred, country, knighthood, all forgot,—
Names that I heed no more, while I possess
Thy heartfelt luxury of loveliness ! "

That summer night had all the healthy cool
That nerves the spirit of the youthful year ;
Yet, as to eyes long fixed on a deep pool,
The waters dark and bright at once appear,
So, through the freshness, on his senses soon
Came the warm memo'ries of the lusty noon.

Such active pleasure tingling through his veins,
Quicken'd his pace beneath the colonnade,
Chesnut, and ilex—to the moonèd plains
A bronze relief and garniture of shade,—
When, just before him, flittingly, he heard
The tender voice of that familiar bird.

Holding his own, to catch that sweeter breath,
And listening, so that each particular sound
Was merged in that attention's depth, his path
Into the secret of the forest wound :
The clear-drawn landscape, and the orb's full gaze,
Gave place to dimness and the wild-wood's maze.

That thrilling sense, which to the weak is fear,
Becomes the joy and guerdon of the brave ;
So, trusting his harmonious pioneer,
His heart he freely to the venture gave,
And through close brake, and under pleachèd aisle,
Walked without sign of outlet many a mile.

When, turning round a thicket weariedly,
A building, of such mould as well might pass
From graceful Greece to conquering Italy,
Rose in soft outline from the silver'd grass,
Whose doors thrown back and inner lustre show'd
It was no lorn and tenantless abode.

T 2

Children of all varieties of fair,
And gaily vested, cluster'd round the portal,
Until one Boy, who had not mien and air
Of future manhood but of youth immortal,
Within an arch of light, came clear to view,
Descending that angelic avenue.

" Stranger ! the mistress of this happy bower,"
Thus the bright messenger the knight addrest—
" Bids us assert her hospitable power,
And lead thee in a captive or a guest ;
Rest is the mate of night,—let opening day
Speed thee rejoicing on thy work and way."

Such gentle bidding might kind answer earn ;
The full moon's glare put out each guiding star ;
He summ'd the dangers of enforc'd return,
And now first marvell'd he had roved so far :
Then murmur'd glad acceptance, tinged with fear,
Lest there unmeet his presence should appear.

Led by that troop of youthful innocence,
A hall he traversed, up whose heaven-topt dome
Thick vapours of delightful influence
From gold and alabaster altars clomb,
And through a range of pillar'd chambers past,
Each one more full of faerie than the last.

To his vague gaze those peopled walls disclosed
Graces and grandeurs more to feel than see,—
Celestial and heroic forms composed
In many a frame of antique poesy ;
But, wheresoe'er the scene or tale might fall,
Still Venus was the theme and crown of all.

There young Adonis scorn'd to yield to her,
Soon by a sterner nature overcome ;
There Paris, happy hapless arbiter,
For beauty barter'd kingdom, race, and home ;
Save what Æneas rescued by her care,
As the Didonian wood-nymph pictured there.

But ere he scanned them long, a Lady enter'd,
In long white robes majestical array'd,
Though on her face alone his eyes were centred,
Which weird suspicion to his mind convey'd,
For every feature he could there divine
Of the old marble in the sylvan shrine.

On his bewilderment she gently smiled,
To his confusion she benignly spoke ;
And all the fears that started up so wild
Lay down submissive to her beauty's yoke :
It was with him as if he saw through tears
A countenance long-loved and lost for years.

She asked, " if so he will'd," the stranger's name,
And, when she heard it, said, " the gallant sound
Had often reached her on the wing of fame,
Though long recluse from fortune's noisy round ;
Her lot was cast in loneliness, and yet
On noble worth her woman-heart was set."

Rare is the fish that is not meshed amain,
When Beauty tends the silken net of praise ;
Thus little marvel that in vaunting strain
He spoke of distant deeds and brave affrays,
Till each self-glorious thought became a charm,
For her to work against him to his harm.

Such converse of melodious looks and words
Paused at the call of other symphonies,
Invisi'ble agencies that draw the cords
Of massive curtains, rising as they rise,
So that the music's closing swell reveal'd
The Paradise of pleasure there conceal'd.

It was a wide alcove, thick-wall'd with flowers,
Gigantic blooms, of aspect that appear'd
Beyond the range of vegetative powers,
A flush of splendour almost to be fear'd,
A strange affinity of life between
Those glorious creatures and that garden's Queen.

Luminous gems were weaving from aloft
Fantastic rainbows on the fountain spray,—
Cushions of broider'd purple, silken-soft,
Profusely heaped beside a table lay,
Whereon all show of form and hue increast
The rich temptation of the coming feast.

There on one couch, and served by cherub hands,
The Knight and Lady banqueted in joy:
With freshest fruits from scarce discover'd lands,
Such as he saw in pictures when a boy,
And cates of flavours excellent and new,
That to the unpalled taste still dearer grew.

Once, and but once, a spasm of very fear
Went through him, when a breeze of sudden cold
Sigh'd, like a dying brother, in his ear,
And made the royal flowers around upfold
Their gorgeous faces in the leafy band,
Like the mimosa touched by mortal hand.

Then almost ghastly seem'd the tinted sheen,
Saltless and savourless those luscious meats,
Till quick the Lady rose, with smile serene,
As one who could command but still entreats,
And filling a gold goblet, kissed the brim,
And passed it bubbling from her lips to him.

At once absorbing that nectareous draught,
And the delicious radiance of those eyes,
At doubt and terror-fit he inly laughed,
And grasped her hand as 'twere a tourney's prize ;
And heard this murmur, as she nearer drew,
" Yes, I am Love, and Love was made for you ! "

They were alone : the' attendants, one by one,
Had vanished : faint and fainter rose the air
Oppressed with odours : through the twilight shone
The glory of white limbs and lustrous hair,
Confusing sight and spirit, till he fell,
The will-less, mindless, creature of the spell.

In the dull deep of satisfied desire
Not long a priso'ner lay that knightly soul,
But on his blood, as on a wave of fire,
Uneasy fancies rode without control,
Voices and phantoms that did scarcely seem
To take the substance of an order'd dream.

At first he stood beside a public road,
Hedged in by myrtle and embower'd by plane,
While figures, vested in old Grecian mode,
Drew through the pearly dawn a winding train,
So strangely character'd, he could not know
Were it of triumph or funereal woe.

For crowns of bay enwreath'd each beauteous head,
Beauty of perfect maid and perfect man ;
Slow-paced the milk-white oxen garlanded ;
Torch-bearing children mingled as they ran
Gleaming amid the elder that uphold
Tripods and cups and plates of chasèd gold.

But then he marked the flowers were colourless,
Crisp-wither'd hung the honourable leaves,
And on the faces sat the high distress
Of those whom Self sustains when Fate bereaves :
So gazed he, wondering how that pomp would close,
When the dream changed, but not to his repose.

For now he was within his father's hall,
No tittle changed of form or furniture,
But all and each a grave memorial
Of youthful days, too careless to endure,—
There was his mother's housewife-work, and there,
Beside the fire, his grandame's crimson chair :

Where, cower'ing low, that ancient woman sat,
Her bony fingers twitching on her knee,
Her dry lips muttering fast he knew not what,
Only the sharp convulsion could he see ;
But, as he looked, he felt a conscience dim
That she was urging God in prayer for him.

Away in trembling wretchedness he turn'd,
And he was in his leman's arms once more ;
Yet all the jewell'd cressets were out-burn'd,
And all the pictured walls, so gay before,
Show'd, in the glimmer of one choking lamp,
Blotched with green mould and worn by filthy damp.

Enormous bats their insolent long wings
Whirl'd o'er his head, and swung against his brow,
And shrieked—" We cozen'd with our ministerings
The foolish knight, and have our revel now : "
And worms bestrew'd the weeds that overspread
The floor with silken flowers late carpeted.

His sick astonished looks he straight addressed
To her whose tresses lay around his arm,
And fervent breath was playing on his breast,
To seek the meaning of this frightful charm ;
But she was there no longer, and instead,
He was the partner of a Demon's bed,—

That, slowly rising, brought the lurid glare
Of its fixed eyes close opposite to his ;
One scaly hand laced in his forehead hair,
Threate'ning his lips with pestilential kiss,
And somewise in the fiendish face it wore,
He traced the features he did erst adore.

With one instinctive agony he drew
His sword, that Palestine remember'd well,
And, quick recoiling, dealt a blow so true,
That down the devi'lish head in thunder fell :—
The effort seem'd against a jutting stone
To strike his hand, and then he woke—alone !

Alone he stood amid those ruins old,
His treas'ury of sweet care and pleasant pain ;
The hemlock crushed defined the body's mould
Of one who long and restless there had lain ;
His vest was beaded with the dew of dawn,
His hand fresh-blooded, and his sword fresh drawn !

The eastern star, a crystal eye of gold,
Full on the statued form of Beauty shone,
Now prostrate, powerless, featureless and cold,
A simple trunk of deftly carven stone:
Deep in the grasses that dismember'd head
Lay like the relics of the' ignoble dead.

But Beauty's namesake and sidereal shrine
Now glided slowly down that pallid sky,
Near and more near the thin horizon line,
In the first gush of morning, there to die,—
While the poor Knight, with wilder'd steps and brain,
Hasten'd the glimme'ring village to regain.

With few uncertain words and little heed
His followers' anxious questions he put by,
Bidding each one prepare his arms and steed,
For "they must march before the sun was high,
And neither Apennine nor Alp should stay,
Though for a single night, his homeward way."

On, on, with scanty food and rest he rode,
Like one whom unseen enemies pursue,
Urging his favou'rite horse with cruel goad,
So that the lagging servants hardly knew
Their master of frank heart and ready cheer,
In that lone man who would not speak or hear.

Till when at last he fairly saw behind
The Alpine barrier of perennial snow,
He seem'd to heave a burthen off his mind,—
His blood in calmer current seem'd to flow,
And like himself he smiled once more, but cast
No light or colour on that cloudy past.

From the old Teuton forests, echoing far,
Came a stern welcome, hailing him restored
To the true health of life in peace or war,
Fresh morning toil, that earns the generous board ;
And waters, in the clear unbroken voice
Of childhood, spoke—" Be thankful and rejoice ! "

Glad as the dove returning to his ark
Over the waste of universal sea,
He heard the huge house-dog's familiar bark,
He traced the figure of each friendly tree,
And felt that he could never part from this
His home of daily love and even bliss.

And in the quiet closure of that place,
He soon his first affection linked anew,
In that most honest passion finding grace,
His soul with primal vigour to endue,
And crush the memories that at times arose,
To stain pure joy and trouble high repose.

Never again that dear and dangerous land,
So fresh with all her weight of time and story,
Her winterless delights and slumbers bland,
On thrones of shade, amid a world of glory,
Did he behold : the flashing cup could please
No longer him who knew the poison-lees.

So lived he, pious, innocent, and brave,
The best of friends I ever saw on earth :
And now the uncommunicable grave
Has closed on him and left us but his worth ;
I have revealed this strange and secret tale
Of human fancy and the powers of bale.

He told it me, one autumn evening mild,
Sitting, greyhair'd, beneath an old oak tree,
His dear true wife beside him, and a child,
Youngest of many, dancing round his knee,—
And bade me, if I would, in fragrant rhymes
Embalm it, to be known in after-times.

THE END.

BRADBURY AND EVANS, PRINTERS, WHITEFRIARS.

CPSIA information can be obtained
at www.ICGtesting.com
Printed in the USA
BVOW06*0843240417
482097BV00006B/27/P